THE PLAYERS AND THEIR PERSONALITIES

Understanding People Who Get
Involved in Addictive
Relationships

TERENCE T. GORSKI

Based on the CENAPS Model of Treatment

Herald House/Independence Press
3225 South Noland Road
P.O. Box 1770
Independence, MO 64055-0770
1-800-767-8181
816/252-5010

ISBN 0-8309-0553-7

Printed in the United States of America

96 95 94 93   3 4 5 6

Table of Contents

Preface

The Game of Love

To form a relationship is to enter into a game complete with rules and strategies. The problem is that most people don't recognize love relationships as games. They don't realize they can choose to play or not to play. Neither do they recognize that different players at the game of love use different sets of rules. To succeed at the game of love, it is important to know what game you and your partner are playing and what rules you are following. If the two of you are not playing the same game, or if you are playing by different rules, it is easy to get trapped in an addictive love relationship.

Addictive love relationships bind people together with intense feelings. These irrational bonds are difficult to break because they are deeply rooted in the personalities of both partners. In this book I will describe the two types of personalities that interact in an addictive relationship and their motivations to get involved and stay involved.

Two players are involved in addictive love relationships: counterdependents and codependents. The counterdependent player appears secure and independent while hiding a secret self that is insecure and fearful. The codependent player appears to be insecure and dependent while hiding a secret self that is controlling and manipulative.

These opposite personalities attract because they complement and fulfill each other. Counterdependents are grandiose, independent, self-centered, and intrusive. In order to function they need codependent partners who are insecure, dependent, other-centered, and lack boundaries. Codependents, in turn, need partners with counterdependent traits. These four interlocking personality traits bind counterdependents and codependents together.

There is hope. It is possible to change and become a person who no longer needs an addictive relationship to feel complete. In this book I will show how to look at the players and the rules they follow in acting out addictive love. I will challenge you to look at yourself and your current and past partners. And most importantly, I will challenge you to change yourself into a person who is capable of healthy love.

Introduction

The Story of the Snake

There once was a man who while walking in the woods found a poisonous snake that was frozen stiff as a board. He knew it was poisonous, but he took pity on the poor frozen thing and brought it home with him. He put the snake in front of the fireplace in his living room so it would thaw out. Realizing that when the snake woke up it would be hungry, the man went to the kitchen and warmed up a bowl of milk so the snake would have something to eat. He then brought the milk back into the living room to feed the snake.

As the man was putting the bowl of milk in front of the snake, it lashed out and bit him. He could feel the venom rush up the veins in his arm and knew he would be dead in a matter of minutes.

With his last strength the man looked at the snake and asked, "Snake, why did you bite me? I found you frozen in the woods. I brought you into my home and thawed you out. I gave you warm milk to drink. Why did you bite me?"

As the man was fading into death he heard the snake hiss these words: "Stop your whining. You knew I was a poisonous snake when you picked me up. What did you expect me to do, kiss you?"

What has this story of the snake got to do with addictive relationships? Have you ever met someone you knew would hurt you? Although part of you said, "Don't get involved," you didn't listen. You let your emotions override your brain and then got hurt? Have you ever been in a relationship that was destroying you?

You knew you needed to get out of it but you just couldn't?

These are all examples of "picking up the snake." An addictive relationship is like a poisonous snake waiting to bite you with its emotional venom. It's a strange snake, however. Before the poison kills, it ignites feelings of passion and sexuality. The poison feels so good at first that it is hard to listen to the rational part of your mind that says "Danger! Stay away! This relationship is poison! You've been here before and you know what is going to happen!" Unfortunately, we often feel compelled to get involved and stay involved in spite of what we know.

This book will help you to understand the "snake" you keep trying to pick up. That snake is an addictive relationship. You need to understand the nature of the addictive relationship to recognize one when you see it. You also need to understand what creates the compulsive need to pick up the snake in the first place and what drives you into the addictive relationship against your rational judgment. Most important, you need to know that you have an alternative. It is possible to learn to say "no" to addictive relationships and learn how to say "yes" to healthy intimacy.

After reading this book you should know what an addictive relationship is and how to recognize it before you get involved. You will know what compels you to get involved and stay involved in spite of the pain and problems. You also will know how to say "no" to addictive relationships and "yes" to healthy relationships.

Chapter 1

Signs and Symptoms of Addictive Relationships

Infatuation—The Intoxicant Emotion that Binds

Chemically dependent and codependent people tend to develop unique relationship styles. For want of a better term we will call these relationships "addictive." Addictive relationships are not identical to chemical addictions, but they are similar in a number of ways.

Addictive relationships produce an intoxicant emotion called infatuation. Like drugs, the feeling of infatuation has the power to change how we think, feel, and act. Drugs change our thinking, feeling, and behavior by changing our brain chemistry. When the drug enters the bloodstream it changes the biological workings of the brain. Because our brain is physically affected we think, feel, and act differently. With continued use mind-altering drugs cause brain dysfunction.

11

> **Addictive relationships have the power to change how we...**
> **think...feel...act...**

Addictive relationships can change moods, but they do it in a different way than mood-altering chemicals. Addictive relationships don't directly poison our brains. They create infatuation which poisons our thoughts and emotions. We begin to believe irrational and magical thoughts that distract us from ourselves and from positive approaches to life and living. We begin listening to our feelings instead of our rational minds. We begin doing things in the name of the relationship that we would never consider doing if we weren't in the relationship.

Addictive relationships distract us from what is wrong with us or our lives. The relationship becomes a central focus, then an obsession. Other things seem to disappear or become insignificant by comparison. The relationship is so important that nothing else counts. As a result, we think about the relationship constantly, even when it would be better to think about other things. Thinking about the relationship allows us to block out other thoughts. This is convenient, especially if we have problems that we would rather not think about.

A codependent woman named Joyce had been divorced for four years and had never been able to get her life together. She was an executive secretary and hated it. She had few friends and was constantly depressed.

Instead of working at solving these problems, all she

ever thought about was men and relationships. She spent a lot of time thinking about how wonderful life would have been if her alcoholic husband hadn't left her. She was shattered by her loneliness and obsessed with finding "the right man." Whenever she was in a relationship she became obsessed with it. She kept getting herself lost in the shuffle of intimacy.

Addictive relationships not only allow us to change how we think, they also allow us to change our feelings. The unique combination of passion and sexuality provides an intense emotional high that blocks out or distorts other feelings. We feel euphoric, like "all is right in the world." In short, we feel in love. But it really isn't love; the term infatuation usually is more appropriate.

What is infatuation? It's a state of temporary insanity marked by intense euphoria and the inability to see our partner realistically. Notice the combination! Euphoria plus the inability to think rationally about our partner.

When we become infatuated we have blinders on. Our minds shut down and we do our thinking with other parts of our anatomy. The actions of our hormones substitute for those of our minds. When we allow our hormones to do our thinking, we're bound to get into trouble in the long run.

> *Infatuation: a state of temporary insanity marked by*
>   - *intense euphoria*
>   - *inability to think clearly, logically, or rationally about your partner*

A man named Jim was recovering from alcoholism and cocaine dependency. He was constantly unhappy in recovery. Something inside him seemed to be driving and pushing him all the time.

He called it "free floating compulsion." He constantly needed to do something—anything—that would make that feeling go away. He didn't like going to AA meetings or counseling because he was forced to think and talk about that free floating compulsion. Also he was challenged to think of sober, rational ways to cope with this feeling without using alcohol or drugs. This made him uncomfortable.

The only thing he could find in sobriety that had the power to make the free floating compulsion go away was Joyce. The passion and intensity of their relationship blotted out all other feelings. She filled him up and made him feel complete. She was so sexual and passionate that she could "blow his mind" on demand. Sex with Joyce was so intense that he felt drained and exhausted in the aftermath. To use his words, "I would merge into a cloud of orgasmic dust and then gently settle back to earth."

Joyce became the center of Jim's newfound recovery. Why? Because she was the only thing that could make his pain and emptiness go away. That's what love is all about—or at least Jim thought so: "How could something that feels so good be bad for me?"

This book is written to help you understand why a relationship like the one between Jim and Joyce is not love.

Intensity—the Goal of Addictive Love

The primary goal of the addictive relationship is to experience intense passion. We think we are in love with our partner, but in reality we are in love with how our partner makes us feel. There's a big difference between the two. In addictive love our respect and love for our partner is not centered on who he or she is as a person but on how that person makes us feel.

As a result, we can easily begin to use partners like a drug by insisting that they make us feel good on demand. This "blow my mind on demand" mentality is one of the crucial hallmarks of an addictive relationship.

The intensity in the addictive relationship is caused by a combination of four different factors: sexuality, anticipation, affirmation, and danger. I use the acronym SAAD to describe these characteristics.

Intensity is caused by...
S = Sexuality
A = Anticipation
A = Affirmation
D = Danger

The "S" stands for **sexuality.** In the early stages of the addictive relationship both partners either feel or pretend to feel an intense feeling of sexual excitement for their partner. In some addictive relationships both partners experience intense sexuality. In others, one

15

partner experiences intense sexual feelings while the other partner pretends to reciprocate to make the relationship work.

This is what happened with Jim and Joyce. The primary feature that attracted Jim to Joyce was the intense sexuality of their relationship. Joyce usually enjoyed their sexual activities and was willing to meet Jim's needs, but having sex was not the main attraction for her. As a matter of fact, she sometimes felt burdened by it and believed Jim was more interested in having sex than he was in her. She was locked into the relationship for other reasons.

This is where **anticipation,** the first "A" in SAAD, comes in. In the early stages of the addictive relationship, both partners believe their partner can make them feel whole or complete. They believe this relationship will "fix" them, and they look forward with great anticipation to being fulfilled and somehow transformed. At a core level they expect their partner will be able to meet needs that no one else has ever met. This anticipation creates tremendous intensity.

It was the anticipation of being made whole, complete, or worthwhile that hooked Joyce into the relationship with Jim and allowed her to tolerate his constant demands for high-intensity sex. She never thought she could attract a man like Jim. It was unbelievable to her that the relationship was real, and she felt she was living a fantasy. Now that she had Jim, Joyce believed her life would be fixed.

The second "A" in SAAD stands for **affirmation.** In the early stages of addictive relationships, both partners are "turned on and tuned in" to each other. They are obsessed with each other and meeting each others needs. They want their partner to love them, so they are always on their best behavior. They affirm and openly tell each other how wonderful they are. This is often the first affirmation either partner has received, and it produces an intense emotional high.

Jim and Joyce were devoted to each other in the early days of their relationship. Jim was focused on Joyce's passion and sexuality. He constantly told her how wonderful and sexy she was. Joyce, who had never felt she was very attractive, was ecstatic about Jim's praise.

The "D" in SAAD stands for **danger**. Danger causes an adrenaline rush that creates excitement, and most addictive relationships have some element of danger. At the very least, a secret bond of "you and me against the world" is formed. In its extreme form, real danger is present. This danger can be caused by such things as having sex in public or semipublic places or falling in love with someone who is married or viewed as dangerous or unacceptable by friends or family.

Jim was a recovering alcoholic. Joyce was recently divorced from an alcoholic who had been physically abusive to her. Although Jim was sober and attending AA meetings, Joyce wasn't sure his recovery would last. She said that this "put an edge on the relationship" and made it kind of exciting.

Addictive Love Defined

Simply defined, an addictive relationship is intensity without substance. Both partners share intense feelings

17

without sharing a broad base of other values, life-style preferences, or mutually respected traits. The intense passion makes both partners feel better without forcing them to think or act better. The relationship is used to avoid thinking clearly, logically, and rationally and as an excuse to act irresponsibly. The relationship allows both partners to temporarily feel better without having to think or act better.

Which Formula Do You follow???

Addictive Relationship	**= Passion – Compatibility**
Healthy Relationship	**= Compatibility + Passion**

Jim and Joyce had an addictive relationship. They had little in common except for the intense feelings they experienced when together. Their relationship was so intense, however, that they didn't have to think about that. They could focus on their pleasure and forget about everything else.

The addictive relationship is very different from a healthy relationship. A healthy relationship can be intense, but the intensity is not the key or central aspect of the relationship. The healthy relationship revolves around a variety of shared values, life-style preferences, and mutually respected traits.

In the healthy relationship the partner is valued as a

human being more highly than the intense feelings. Passion and sexuality, although important, are secondary features. They are enjoyed for what they are and kept in an appropriate place. The relationship does not substitute for clear, logical, and rational thinking or for responsible behavior.

Addictive relationships give both partners the ability to turn off their minds. It allows them to turn off painful and uncomfortable feelings by replacing them with infatuation and passion. This is especially appealing to people who were taught to "not think" and "not feel" as children. It is why people who were raised in alcoholic or dysfunctional homes are likely to develop addictive relationships as adults.

Addictive relationships also give both partners permission to act in new and novel ways. People in addictive relationships often do things they would never do if they weren't in the relationship. Some of these things are positive. The relationship often gives us permission to be more caring, concerned, and passionate. We may learn to value other people to a greater degree than we ever have before. Sometimes we find a positive side to ourselves that we never knew existed.

Jim put it like this: "I've never really noticed anyone before. I never realized that I could make someone else as important in my life as I have made Joyce. I think this is the first time in my sobriety I have ever acted as if another person really counts."

Unfortunately, addictive relationships also produce negative and painful consequences. The relationship feels so good and assumes such a high priority in our lives that we ignore other people and things. Close friends often are abandoned or important responsibilities are ignored. The relationship may also cause new problems like jealousy or obsession with controlling our partner's reactions to us.

The relationship may invite us to act irresponsibly. We feel like kids again, and when we feel like kids it's easy to act like kids. Unfortunately children often behave irresponsibly and get into trouble because of it. When our emotions are running our lives it's easy to overreact and make "feeling good" our number one priority.

Jim reflected the negative aspects when he said, "I just don't have time for the things I used to do. I'm taking time away from work to be with Joyce. I hope I don't get caught, but I really don't care. I'm also spending more money than I should and I'm missing AA meetings. I haven't talked to my sponsor in weeks, but I feel like I don't need him anymore. This relationship is so special that I feel like a different person. She's so good for me I can't see that there is anything wrong with what I'm doing."

In a nutshell, people recovering from chemical dependency and codependency often get into dysfunctional relationships. Because these relationships have the power to change their moods, just like alcohol and other drugs used to, they are called addictive relationships.

Addictive relationships bring intense feelings of passion caused by a combination of sexuality, anticipation, affirmation, and danger. The relationship makes both partners feel a "high" or a "charge." But there are few if any other shared values, goals, or life-style preferences. When the passion is gone, little else is left.

20

In spite of this, the relationship seems magical because it gives both partners permission to change how they think, what they feel, and how they act. Some of the changes are positive; others are negative. The very nature of the addictive relationship creates pain and struggle.

Both partners tend to internalize these negative changes. They come to believe that the negative things are happening to them because they are bad or they are not good enough. They also credit all of the positive outcomes to the relationship. They say to themselves, "I'm not responsible for the good things that are happening—our relationship is. If the relationship ends, all of the good things will disappear."

In the long run, addictive relationships weaken us and healthy relationships strengthen us. Essentially, it is how the partners interact with each other that provides a bond of growing strength or progressive destruction. The nature of the relationship in large part is determined by the players' personalities.

Chapter 2

The Players

To form a relationship is to enter into a game complete with rules and strategies. The problem is that most people don't recognize love relationships as games. As a result they don't realize they can choose to play or not to play. They also don't recognize that different players at the game of love use different sets of rules. To succeed at love it is important to know what game your partner is playing and what rules he or she is following. Let's look at the players and the rules they follow in acting out an addictive relationship.

The Magic Triad: You, Me, and Us

All relationships require two players—you and me. Once we start to relate with one another, a third entity is created—us. So in reality all relationships are triangles consisting of You (who you are as a person), Me (who I am as a person), and Us (the relationship that develops as we interact with each other).

When relationships become problematic it is helpful to separate the problems into three categories: your problems (the problems associated with who you are as a person), my problems (the problems associated with who I am as a person), and our problems (the relationship problems we share which are created by how we communicate and interact with one another).

All three members of this triangle—you, me, and us—are important. Our primary focus, however, is going to be on the type of people who come together to create the addictive relationship. The important questions to answer are these: Who am I and what kind of a relationship do I have a tendency to create? Who is my partner and what type of relationship does he or she have a tendency to create? By understanding our own motivations and those of our partners we can begin to understand why certain types of relationships just seem to happen. Only then can we learn how to change them!

> *First the self*
> *Then the possibility*
> *For healthy love*

People in addictive relationships want the relationship to magically fix them and solve all of their problems.

They want the relationship to change without having to change anything else. If they don't need somebody else to fix them, they are less likely to be seduced into an addictive relationship. This is why they need to re-claim themselves first. Then, and only then, will it be possible to create healthy intimate relationships. First the self, then the possibility of intimacy. With this in mind let's look at the individuals who come together to create the addictive relationship.

The Players—Counterdependents and Codependents

There are two players in the addictive relationship: the counterdependent and the codependent. The counter-dependent is a person who outwardly appears secure and independent but privately insecure and fearful. Codependents appear insecure and seek to lose them-selves in others. Underneath, however, they are often strong, capable people. Codependents are afraid of their strength so they channel it into taking care of others. And to properly care for someone else, they are not above attempting to control and manipulate.

The best-known player in the addictive relationship is the codependent, who is continually fearful of being abandoned. Codependents believe their role in life is to take care of others. At the same time they believe they need the approval and care of others. The stronger the person who approves and cares for them the better. They are willing to lose themselves in someone else to get the approval and support that they believe they need.

Codependents believe themselves to be inadequate

and insecure, and they present this image to the world. Underneath they are usually strong and competent but incapable of seeing this in themselves much less believing it. The idea that they have personal strength and power is so frightening that they allow themselves to get in touch with that power only when they are taking care of someone else.

Codependents spend a lot of time and energy hiding their strengths. They are most comfortable when they see themselves in a supportive role relying on and identifying with someone else's strengths. Codependents can be either men or women. Many codependents become chemically dependent.

Counterdependents overidentify with their feelings of strength, power, and confidence. They repress any awareness of weakness and vulnerability. This is the key to understanding how they operate in life. They believe they will die if they are ever weak or vulnerable. As a result they spend an excessive amount of time and energy becoming, looking, and acting strong. They fear their weakness and will do anything to keep from having to acknowledge limitations.

Codependents are the opposite of counterdependents in many ways. This is why they fit so well together. Codependents overidentify with the outward appearance of insecurity and inadequacy. They deny any sense of inner strength or power. They feel out of control and unable to influence themselves or others. As a result, they believe they need someone strong and powerful in their lives at all times. They also believe that if they ever act out their strength something awful will happen to them.

This is the key to understanding codependents. They are most comfortable when they perceive themselves to be weak and helpless but in the care of someone who is strong and competent. Getting in touch with their own strength makes them feel crazy. They are afraid that something awful will happen to them if they ever contact and act out their own strength.

This is why counterdependents get involved with codependents. If I were a counterdependent and were to honestly tell you what I found attractive about you as a codependent, I'd say something like this: "I like you because you're really strong enough to take care of me, but I can pretend I'm taking care of myself and controlling you. You'll never challenge me. You'll never directly act out your strength against me. As a result I feel safe. This is why I love you."

Codependents get involved with counterdependents for different reasons. A codependent would say to a counterdependent partner, "I like you because you are going to take care of me. You will make the decisions I am afraid to make. You will keep me protected from other people. You'll make me look good. I can take on your strength as a way to feel good about myself. It's not my strength, but it's better than being totally weak and helpless."

Many people assume that all addicted people are counterdependent and all nonaddicts in relationships with addicts are codependent. This is not always true. There are many addicts who are codependent and many nonaddicts in relationships with addicts who are counterdependent.

Counterdependents and codependents share a number of interlocking traits. Counterdependents are grandiose, and codependents are insecure. Counterdependents are extremely independent, and codependents are extremely dependent. Counterdependents are self-centered, and codependents are other-centered. Counterdependents are intrusive; the codependents are receptive.

Counterdependents	Codependents
Appear to Others	**Appear to Others**
• *Secure*	• *Insecure*
• *Independent*	• *Dependent*
Secretly feels	**Secretly feels**
• *Insecure*	• *Controlling*
• *Fearful*	• *Manipulative*

Because counterdependents and codependents represent polar opposites they complement one another. Counterdependents see a sense of vulnerability in codependents that they can't allow themselves to experience. Codependents see strengths in counterdependents that they can't allow themselves to experience. In spite of glaring differences they sense a mysterious attraction.

It is a conflicted attraction, however. Both partners are at war within themselves. They are in a constant state of inner conflict or struggle and believe they need their partner to find inner peace.

> **Conflicted people are at
> war with themselves
> They need another person
> to make peace inside them.**

The counterdependent and codependent are conflicted. Both are at war with themselves, but the object of their battles is different. Counterdependent persons battle to appear strong and in direct control of others. They push down all feelings of weakness. Codependent persons battle to manipulate others subtly by acting weak and helpless. They push down their feelings of strength and competence. Let's look in more depth at both of these players.

Counterdependent players are not well known. Even though their role is obvious, very few people talk about them. Although many people assume that all counterdependent people are men, don't be fooled. There are many women who act out this role in relationships.

Counterdependent partners present themselves as outwardly secure, independent, and confident. Privately they are insecure and require constant support and praise from others. They can't admit to themselves or anyone else that this dependent side of them exists. They spend a lot of time and energy hiding this side of themselves from others.

Now let's explore these interlocking traits in more detail.

Chapter 3

The Personalities and How They Relate

The personalities of counterdependents and codependents lock into each other, and as a result they need each other. Counterdependents act out four primary characteristics: grandiosity, extreme independence, self-centeredness, and intrusiveness. Codependents act out four opposite and complementary traits: insecurity, overdependence, other-centeredness, and a lack of boundaries. These traits lock into and complement each other. When we don't have a partner to counterbalance our traits, we can't function very well. This is what is meant by the terms dependent or symbiotic relationship.

Each primary trait has a number of secondary characteristics. Let's review these primary traits and their secondary characteristics to see exactly how they lock into each other.

Grandiosity and Insecurity

The first set of interlocking traits involves the grandiosity of the counterdependent and the insecurity of the codependent. Counterdependents are grandiose. They need partners who allow them to maintain their illusion of strength and power. Codependents are insecure. They feel incomplete and inadequate. They need strong partners who can make them feel complete and competent. Here is the attraction. The grandiosity of the counterdependent needs the insecurity of the codependent and vice versa.

Both grandiosity and insecurity are based on low self-esteem. People who have low self-esteem believe they can't cope with life and don't deserve the good things life has to offer. If we feel this way about ourselves we

32

can cope with it in one of three ways.

The counterdependent strategy focuses on and exaggerates strengths while denying and blocking out weaknesses. We build our self-identity around our strengths and come to believe that any sign of weakness will destroy our image of who we are. As a result we exaggerate and overidentify with our strengths while minimizing and disowning any weaknesses. This leads to grandiosity. When we become grandiose, we delude ourselves into believing that we are stronger and more powerful than we really are.

The codependent strategy focuses on and exaggerates weaknesses while denying or blocking out awareness of strengths. We build our self-identity around our weaknesses and come to believe that any sign of inner strength or power will destroy us. As a result we exaggerate and overidentify with our weaknesses while minimizing or disowning our strengths. This leads to insecurity. We delude ourselves into believing that we are weaker and more helpless than we really are.

The third strategy is the healthy one. We can learn to accept ourselves as we are with all of our strengths *and* weaknesses. When we accept our strengths we can use them to help ourselves and others. When we recognize and accept our weaknesses we can ask for help and allow others to help us. In this way we can grow. We can use our strengths to either overcome or compensate for our weaknesses. Because we are secure in who we are, we can show both our strengths and weaknesses to others without shame or guilt. We are free to be who we really are with all our strengths and weaknesses.

It's important to see how the grandiosity and in-security lock into each other. Why? Because this is one of the four major locks that traps us into addictive relationships. Study the following diagram for a moment:

Grandiosity	*Insecurity*
Powerful	*Ineffectual*
Self-confident	*Uncertain*
Self-important	*Insignificant*
Entitled	*Deprived*
One-of-a-kind	*None-of-a-kind*

The sense of power in the counterdependent locks into the codependent's feelings of being ineffectual. The counterdependent and codependent make a silent agreement: "I won't challenge your power if you don't challenge me when I blame all my problems on being ineffectual." In this way they enable each other to stay sick. They refuse to make each other's problems visible or to challenge one another to learn and grow.

The same is true of the other traits. The high self-confidence of the counterdependent locks into the un-certainty of the codependent. The counterdependent says, "I need you to believe in my strength and en-courage me in my grandiose thinking." The counter-dependent responds, "Of course I will. I can't really do much on my own. By being involved with you at least I can accomplish something."

The exaggerated self-importance of the counterdependent locks into the insignificance of the codependent. The counterdependent says, "I am more important than you or anyone else." The codependent says, "Of course you are! I'm insignificant in comparison to you. I'm just grateful that you allow me to stay around."

The entitlement of the counterdependent locks into the sense of deprivation of the codependent. The counterdependent says, "I have a right to expect you to serve me." The codependent says, "Of course you do! I was raised to be a servant, and it's only right I should take care of you. I don't have a right to expect anything more from my own life."

The one-of-a-kind thinking of the counterdependent locks into the none-of-a-kind thinking of the codependent. The counterdependent says, "I am special and unique. I need you to recognize that." The codependent says "I know you are special, and I need your specialness because I am nothing."

Let's look in more detail at the secondary characteristics of grandiosity and insecurity that lock the counterdependent and codependent players together.

Grandiosity

Counterdependents are grandiose. They have an exaggerated sense of self-importance. Grandiose people share a number of traits in common.

Powerful. Grandiosity causes us to feel powerful, and this sense of power sets our imaginations to work. We develop power fantasies. We become preoccupied with the private belief that we are or will become power-ful and influential. For the most part, our satisfaction is in the power fantasy itself not in the actual achieve-ment. This is why so many grandiose people accom-plish little or nothing but still keep their grandiosity intact. When we do accomplish something, the real achievement is usually disappointing. As counterdepen-dents we tend to think: "If I can do it it must not be worth much." The antidote to our disappointment is to create an even more grandiose power fantasy to distract us from reality and allow us to reenter the world of magical thinking.

As a result of their power fantasies, many counter-dependents set unrealistically high goals for them-selves. They want to be perfect or ideal people acting out or reaching toward impossibly high goals. They are preoccupied with fantasies of striving for and attaining perfect wisdom, beauty, and ideal love. As a result, they often are susceptible to the teachings of gurus who tell them that they are "god" and can become perfect or all powerful.

Self-confident. Counterdependents feel self-confident. This can be a positive trait when it cor-responds with reality, but many counterdependents carry it to extremes. They often feel confidence when by right they should feel frightened or insecure. The film "Butch Cassidy and the Sundance Kid" dramatizes this sense of unwarranted self-confidence and the danger it causes.

Butch and Sundance are trapped by hundreds of Mexican troops. They weave a grandiose plan of escape

36

and then run out to be killed by a hail of bullets after convincing themselves that they can make it. This is how many counterdependents live their lives. They weave elaborate schemes of control and manipulation that blow up in their faces and create problems.

Self-important. Counterdependents have an exaggerated sense of their own importance. They consciously believe that they are more important than they really are while unconsciously believing that they are not important enough. To make themselves feel more important, they diminish the importance of others. They will put others down at every opportunity just to make themselves look and feel good. Obviously, they enjoy exerting power and influence over others.

Entitled. Counterdependents feel entitled to special benefits or treatment without doing much in return. They unreasonably expect other people to give them special consideration even though they have done little to earn it.

One-of-a-kind. Counterdependents believe they are special or "one-of-a-kind" and that they can be understood only by other special or privileged people. This causes them to see their friends and family members in an idealized fashion. Any time friends or family members present themselves as fallible human beings, the counterdependent tends to lose respect for them. They either put others on a pedestal and worship them or they judge them harshly and want nothing to do with them. Others are either wonderful or terrible; there is no middle ground. This is known as black-or-white or all-or-none thinking.

How the Codependent Fits in. We might think that the counterdependent would have difficulty finding a partner who would be willing to tolerate such grandiosity, but this isn't the case. Codependents love their counterdependent partner's grandiosity. They believe their partner is important! They communicate things like, "You're very special. You're unique. You say you don't trust me, but I know you don't mean it. I can see beneath your grandiosity to the loving, caring person that you are. I—and only I—am capable of bringing out those loving and caring traits whether you want me to or not." Codependents think and say these things because they have a set of opposite but compatible traits based on insecurity.

Insecurity

Codependents are insecure and believe they can't make it in life without someone else taking care of or supporting them. They don't believe they are able to function alone in the world or enjoy the benefits of life. In the codependent this insecurity causes a need or a compulsion to fix or take care of someone else. It's OK to work hard for others, but they can't work hard for themselves. Why? Because they really don't believe they are worthy of having success or good things in life. The best they can hope to do is to make those things available for someone else.

Their insecurity sets codependents up to be victimized by others. Because they believe that they can't make it in life and must take care of others, they become willing to enslave themselves to someone who is stronger and more capable. They believe they can get rid of their constant fear and insecurity by hooking up with someone who is stronger. Unfortunately, this generally doesn't work because they hook up with people who victimize or abandon them, often ending up hurt and alone without understanding why. So they blame themselves by saying things like, "I didn't try hard enough! If I would have done more or been something different he would not have left me!"

This insecurity has a number of characteristics that include the following:

Ineffectual. Codependents feel they can't do anything right. They try to take care of this feeling by fixing others. Their need to fix or take care of others can turn into a compulsion. They believe that if they can get good enough at fixing others, this sense of being ineffectual will go away. Of course, this never happens, and they end up being exploited and victimized by others.

Codependents believe their job is to rescue people and to be there to meet the needs of everyone at all times. They learn to meet other people's needs without being asked. They consistently give more than they receive and believe that it is good and noble to do so. They fix other peoples' feelings. They do the thinking for others and then give away the credit. They are willing to suffer other people's consequences. All this they do with a sense of gratitude: "Thank you for letting me suffer this way." Their only reward is in helping others achieve impossible dreams: "If I can make him (or her) a success, then my life will have meaning and purpose."

Codependents romanticize their caretaking by creating fantasies of becoming the perfect helper or stoic victim. They see themselves as noble martyrs to the cause of other peoples' well-being. These fantasies give them a sense of meaning and purpose.

Joyce had a number of perfect-helper fantasies. She would envision Steve getting terribly sick and herself coming to his rescue. At other times she would imagine him getting into serious problems with his career, and after coming to her for help she saved the day.

Joyce also had a number of victim fantasies that occupied her mind when she was depressed. She saw herself as a victim stoically enduring abuse and hard times in the name of love. In her fantasies the payoff would be that Steve would love her all the more for her suffering. Her favorite fantasy was to stand at the doorway as Steve was leaving on a business trip and imagine him never coming back because he got killed in an airplane crash.

Because they feel ineffectual, many codependents set unbelievably low goals for themselves. They have difficulty meeting goals that are equal to their real ability. When other people see them as competent or worthwhile they usually are surprised.

Joyce was an executive secretary. She made a good salary and her boss gave her a great deal of decision-making responsibility and freedom. In spite of this she hated the job. "I'm just a secretary," she said. "I can never amount to anything on my own. If it weren't for my boss I wouldn't be able to do anything." In fact, Joyce ran the office, supervised the secretarial staff, and made many key decisions. But she didn't *believe* that she did. She would minimize her decision-making power. When challenged about it, she replied, "OK, so I do make some important decisions, but I don't do it as well as my boss could. I could never make the decisions I make if I didn't know my boss was ultimately responsible." As a result she never asked for a raise or a change in title. She willingly gave away all of the credit to her boss for what she did. "After all," she concluded, "he deserves it and I don't."

Many codependents achieve a great deal in their lives and careers yet in their own eyes they are underachievers. "I'll never be able to do anything on my own," they think. "The best I can hope for is to be allowed to help somebody else."

Uncertain. Codependents lack inner confidence. They feel they can't manage the challenges of life. As a result they spend a lot of time being quietly afraid. They also have low self-worth. They have the feeling they are not worthy of living and have no right to enjoy the good things in life. Unable to take genuine pleasure in their achievements, they feel terrified by their own success and so are more than willing to give the credit to others. Often, codependents are unable to experience genuine pleasure due to a core belief that they are unworthy and incapable.

Insignificant. Codependents spend a great deal of time feeling insignificant. On a deep level they believe they don't really count for much. They feel unimportant and allow other people to treat them that way.

This belief that they are insignificant causes them to feel less capable than other people. They often see themselves as petty little people with no real sense of importance. As a result, they constantly put themselves down and have difficulty receiving compliments. They also tend to question the judgment of anyone who sees them as important.

Deprived. Codependents feel deprived, and in many cases they are. With minimal expectations, they make few demands and receive little from life. They live in emotional poverty and just assume that it has to be that way. They believe they don't deserve much. They have the feeling they are not worthy of living and have little or no right to enjoy the good things that life has to offer. They say things to themselves like, "I don't have any expectations. I am so preoccupied with attending to the needs of others that it doesn't dawn on me that I would want anything for myself. I don't expect anything from anyone else. I'm happy with what I get no matter how little it is. I learned long ago that by expecting or asking for things I would only be disappointed or punished."

This assumption that deprivation is normal gives others permission to do whatever they please. They say, "Do whatever you want, I won't question it. As a matter of fact, I won't even think about it." They act in accordance with these rules: don't think, don't question, don't expect.

None-of-a-kind. Codependents feel they don't belong or fit in anywhere. This leads them to settle for just about anyone as a partner. They also put themselves down by saying things like, "I don't count. I'm not worth much. I'm unworthy. I can't imagine why other people would want to spend time with me. I can't imagine what other people could possibly see in me."

This none-of-a-kind thinking leads to a pleasure deficit. Codependents are unable to take genuine pleasure in their achievements. Terrified by their own success they are more than willing to give the credit to others. The codependents' inability to take genuine pleasure has to do with their core belief that they are unworthy and incapable.

How Counterdependents Lock into Low Self-esteem. Counterdependents take full advantage of their partners' low self-esteem because it feeds their grandiosity. Being involved with partners who feel terrible about themselves makes them feel strong and powerful by comparison. The codependent constantly comes to the counterdependent for help, encouragement, and advice. This feeds the ego of their counterdependent partners who love them for it.

In fact, counterdependents *need* to have codependents to keep their ego inflated. Counterdependents believe they cannot live without this continuous reinforcement from the codependent. The counterdependent has a deep-seated low self-esteem; however it is expressed in a different way than codependents do.

Self-esteem has two components—self-confidence and self-worth. Codependents lack both. They do not feel confident of meeting life's challenges, although in reality they are. And they don't feel worthy of having or enjoying the good things in life.

Counterdependents express their low self-esteem differently. They have high levels of self-confidence and they trust themselves. But like codependents, they lack self-worth. They also believe that they aren't worthy of having or enjoying the good things in life. They believe, "If I can have it, it must not be worth very much."

This shared low self-esteem forms a powerful attraction and bond. Both partners feel they know and can relate to each other on a deep level. In most addictive relationships, both partners believe they have found their "soul mate." When the relationship is explored in depth, both partners share a core of low self-worth that binds them together. Their relationship becomes a refuge from the world that both believe they don't deserve and can't enjoy.

Independence and Dependence

The second set of interlocking traits in addictive relationships involves the extreme independence of the counterdependent and extreme dependence of the co-dependent. Counterdependents rely mostly on themselves and need people who will not demand a relationship on a personal or feeling level. Codependents are extremely dependent. They need someone strong and powerful to take care of them. They need to be needed.

Let's look at how these traits form the second major lock that binds the counterdependent and codependent together. Study the following diagram for a moment.

Independence	Dependence
Trust Self	.......Trust Others
Distrust Others	.......Distrust Self
Over-identify with	.......Over-identify with
Strengths	Weaknesses
Deny Weaknesses	.......Deny Strengths
Demanding	.......Complying
Praise-seeking	.......Approval-seeking

The tendency of counterdependents to trust themselves and distrust others locks into the tendency of codependents to trust others and distrust themselves. The counterdependent says, "I have to do everything myself because no one else can do anything right!" The codependent says "You're right! I know I can't do anything right no matter how hard I try. That's why I rely on you."

The way the counterdependent focuses on and exaggerates personal strengths locks into the way the codependent focuses on and exaggerates personal weaknesses. The counterdependent says, "I am always strong and capable! I have no weaknesses, so stay out of my way." The codependent says, "I need your strength because I am so weak and helpless."

The way the counterdependent demands and imposes expectations on others locks into the way the codependent constantly seeks reassurance from others. The counterdependent says, "I demand that you serve me." The codependent says, "I'll serve you well as long as you constantly reassure me and tell me I am OK."

The way the counterdependent demands to be praised locks into the way the codependent tends to comply. The codependent says, "I'll give you the praise you want if you don't hurt me."

Let's look at each of these traits in more detail.

Extreme Independence

Counterdependents appear to be extremely independent. They rely upon and trust themselves and have a difficult time doing the same with others. This extreme independence is marked by a number of characteristics.

Trust Self. Counterdependents trust themselves. They tend to look to themselves for reinforcement and rely only on themselves to cope with problems. When something goes wrong, they try to fix it by themselves first. They have difficulty asking for help. Jack even had trouble going to a gas station to ask for directions when he got lost in a strange neighborhood. "I can figure it out myself," he would say. "Besides, they probably don't know where it is either."

Distrust of Others. Counterdependents tend to distrust others, focusing on their failings and shortcomings. To justify this belief they ignore or block out others' strong points and successes. They trust only themselves because they know everyone else will just let them down. After all, no one is as strong or competent as they are. They have a difficult time trusting their partners who have let themselves get too close and, therefore, vulnerable. The counterdependent would think something like this, "Because I have given you the power to hurt me, I can never really feel safe around you. Why? Because I have given you the power to hurt me and I believe that you will."

> **We are afraid that others will do to us
> The things that we generally do to them.**

A general rule of human nature is that we are afraid that others will do to us what we generally do to others. Counterdependents are afraid their partners will hurt them. Why? Because they are capable of hurting others and believe that everyone else is like them.

Overidentify with Strengths. Counterdependents overidentify with their strengths. They focus on what they are good at and build their self-identity around it. They also devalue anything that they are not good at. They operate as if things only count if they can do them well. They will only do things that they are good at and are deathly afraid of looking incompetent, weak, or helpless.

As a result, counterdependents constantly are driven to test and prove themselves. For them, life is a competition. They are constantly battling the world and everyone in it.

Deny Weaknesses. Counterdependents are uncomfortable with their weaknesses and limitations. They believe that something awful would happen if other people knew that this part of them existed. Therefore, they hide behind a mask of strength. This low self-esteem in the counterdependent motivates a need to compete with others. They also demand that others pay attention to their strengths and ignore their weaknesses.

Demanding. Counterdependents have high expectations of others and are not afraid to ask them to do things. They get upset easily when their demands aren't met. Counterdependents are demanding of others because they have extremely high demands for themselves. The high demands they put on others set them up for constant disappointment. They frequently say to themselves, "Nobody is capable of doing it right! I knew I was wrong to trust them. I'd be better off doing it by myself."

Praise Seeking. To build their egos counterdependents seek the praise and recognition of others. Underneath this extreme independence they have a low opinion of themselves. They can't enjoy life, and at times they doubt if they can even function well. Much of the time they're afraid and need constant attention and admiration from partners to distract them from their fear.

If they don't get the correct response from one specific person they try to get it from someone else and say, "If they don't recognize how wonderful I am it's their fault and their loss." If counterdependents get negative feedback from others, however, they often react with rage, shame, and humiliation. This is because they deny any personal weakness.

How Codependents Lock into Extreme Independence. Codependents put up with the extreme independence of counterdependents because they can see the weakness and vulnerability that is underneath. This weakness and vulnerability is one of the most appealing things about their partner. The fact that only they can see it makes them feel special and important. They think this way: "I can see all of your fear and insecurity, but don't worry about it. I'm going to change all that and make it better. I'm real sensitive, and I can see other people's feelings even if they can't see them or talk about them. I see your fear but I'm not going to tell you that. I see that little kid in you and that's why I ignore your extreme independence. I know there is a hurt and fragile person inside of you and it's my job to nurture that part of you. I am going to take care of all those things that you can't talk about or take care of yourself."

Extreme Dependence

The second major trait of codependents is overdependence on others. They are extremely dependent. There are a number of characteristics associated with this overdependence.

Trust Others. Codependents have an exaggerated sense of the importance of others. They trust others even when it is irrational to do so. They believe they need to have other people make them OK. They exaggerate the importance of others and minimize their own power and importance. They tend to believe in and trust others while distrusting themselves. They constantly

49

think this way: "You are more important than I am! Whatever you want, you deserve; I deserve nothing. Anything you choose to give me is a special treat for which I am grateful."

Distrust Self. Codependents distrust themselves and turn to others for reinforcement and support. They believe they can't handle the problems of living all by themselves, even though in reality they can. The irony here is that most codependents are quite competent, but their lack of self-trust prevents them from recognizing that fact.

Over-identify with Weaknesses. Codependents focus on and exaggerate their personal weaknesses, and they even build their self-concept around them. They feel a need to be perfect but realize that's impossible—after all anything they accomplish is insignificant: "If a weak person like me can do it, it must not be worth much."

Recently, while I was talking with a friend at an ACA conference, four people ·interrupted me to ask directions. The first three people were codependent. How could I tell? They all said something like this: "Excuse me. I really don't want to interrupt you, and I hate to bother someone as important as you, but I can't find the right conference room. It seems like I'm always getting lost. Could you help me?"

The fourth person either wasn't codependent or else had made a lot of progress in recovery. She simply said, "Excuse me! I need some help in finding the correct conference room. Will you give me directions?"

Deny Strengths. Codependents deny their personal strengths. They block out any awareness that they have the capacity to be strong and capable. Why? They believe it is dangerous to be strong because other people will demand or expect more from them. Most codependents are strong, capable people but don't believe it. Even when given direct positive feedback they devalue it. One codependent once told me, "I used to respect my boss. Then he started telling me what a good job I was doing. How can I respect anyone who has such poor judgment."

Complying. Codependents comply with the wishes of others—they do what they are told. They may not like it, but they generally do it anyway. Codependents are good helpers because they like to help and enjoy being of service. They feel fulfilled when they are rescuing or fixing someone else. They do tasks no one else is willing to do, and when they are done they willingly trade away the credit. If they are given negative feedback they assume it's true without questioning the possibility that it could be wrong. They simply try harder. Why? They believe they need constant reassurance from others and are willing to do just about anything to get it.

Approval Seeking. Codependents constantly want the approval of others. Their rationale goes something like this: "Because I can't approve of myself, I desperately need your help. I've got to know you think I'm OK, and the only way for me to feel OK about who I am is to get your approval. Without it I am nothing, and to get it I am willing to do just about anything you want me to do. I will take care of you so well that you would not possibly consider getting along without me. I will perform so well that you will have to keep me. Please tell me that you want me. Please don't see how inadequate I really am."

How Counterdependents Lock into Extreme Dependence. Counterdependents love the over dependence of the codependent because of their own extreme independence. They need someone who will let them continue to believe they can make it in life all by themselves.

Codependents are the perfect partners for counterdependents. They have someone to depend on, someone who will never attempt to take the credit or make them look bad. They have found a partner who expects little and will not challenge their authority, point out their dependence and inadequacy, or demand more than they are willing to give. Most important in the mind of the counterdependent is the knowledge they have found someone who will not take away their freedom.

Self-centered and Other-centered

The third set of interlocking traits involves the self-centeredness of counterdependents and the other-centeredness of codependents. The self-centeredness of counterdependents motivates them to demand attention and praise. The other-centeredness of the codependent motivates them to give attention and praise to others. Because of their other-centeredness, codependents are oversensitive to the needs of others. They will say or do anything to make their partners feel comfortable. They learn to read between the lines and respond to that which is not spoken about in the relationship. This compensates for counterdependents' self-centeredness.

This entanglement between self-centeredness and other-centeredness forms the third lock that binds the counterdependent and the codependent together. Study the following diagram for a moment.

Self-centered		Other-centered
Insensitive	...	Oversensitive
Selfish	...	Altruistic
Exploitive	...	Nurturing

The insensitivity of the counterdependent locks into the oversensitivity of the codependent. The counterdependent says, "I don't know or care how you feel!" The codependent says, "I know you don't mean that. I can sense the warmth and caring underneath. I know you really love me and have warm, tender feelings inside."

The selfishness of the counterdependent locks into the altruism of the codependent. Altruism means "a willingness to sacrifice self to others." The counterdependent says, "I am all important. You only count if you do what I want and reflect back to me what I want to see!" The codependent says, "I'm really not worth anything. I can see that you are more important so I'll be anything or anyone you want me to be. I'll sacrifice myself to you."

The exploitiveness of the counterdependent locks into the nurturing of the codependent. The counterdependent says, "I count; you don't. You owe me. I have a right to anything that you have." The codependent says, "I love you. I will give you anything that I have. Because of my love, I am willing to sacrifice myself to you."

The tendency of counterdependents to depersonalize others and view them as objects locks into the tendency of codependents to depersonalize themselves and treat themselves as objects. The counterdependent says, "You are an object put here for me to use." The codependent responds, "I know that. I'm not really a person. Please use me and make my life worthwhile."

Let's look at each of these traits in more detail.

Self-centered

Counterdependents are self-centered. This self-centeredness is characterized by a number of traits.

Insensitivity. Counterdependents don't know what other people are feeling and typically don't care because they are preoccupied with their own needs. After all, to notice the feelings of others they would have to recognize their own feelings—and that's too painful! Their attitude toward their partner's feelings is typically, "You can have feelings if you want to, but don't bother me with them. Don't expect me to waste my time dealing with your petty problems."

Selfish. Counterdependents tend to care only about themselves and what they have but are not very concerned about other people. As a result, they do best when they are around people who are good at self-sacrifice. They are also self-centered, believing the world ends at the tip of their nose. Here's a riddle that illustrates this: How many counterdependents does it take to screw in a light bulb? Answer: Only one. They hold the bulb up to the socket and it screws itself in as the world revolves around them.

Exploitive. Counterdependents take advantage of, manipulate, or use other people to achieve their own ends. They see nothing wrong with this. They believe it is the job of other people to take care of them and do what they want. Making demands comes easy for them.

This exploitiveness causes them to depersonalize other people. They view others as things and treat other people like objects to be used to bolster their own self-esteem. Counterdependents are skilled in dealing with things. They have difficulty dealing with real people with feelings and values.

How Codependents Lock into Self-centeredness. Codependents are comfortable with self-centered people because they don't expect empathy, attention, or caring. They find it acceptable for counterdependents to ignore them and their needs. They think this way: "I wouldn't expect you to take care of me. It wouldn't dawn on me that you would be there for me. It's never happened before; why should it start now? It's my job to be here for you. I will be everything you want me to be. Don't worry about me. I'm OK. I don't have any needs. I don't have any feelings that I need to talk about. However you want to feel, I'll help you feel that way. That's how I am able to feel good about myself."

Other-centered

Codependents are preoccupied with the needs of others to their own detriment. They are more concerned with others than they are with themselves. They distract themselves from personal problems by getting overly involved with the needs of others. As a result, they are easily exploited. There are a number of characteristics that accompany this other-centeredness.

Oversensitive. Codependents are often oversensitive to the needs and opinions of others. With empathy in overdrive they are capable of tremendous warmth and personal identification with others. They seem to know intuitively how other people are feeling and what others need.

Altruistic. Codependents are willing to sacrifice themselves for others. In fact, they are generous to the point of hurting themselves. They have difficulty in accumulating things for themselves. In relationships they are comfortable in sharing but can't understand the difference between sharing and giving everything away.

Their altruism makes codependents easy to exploit. They seem to be wearing a sign that says, "Kick me, use me, take advantage of me." They often invite exploitation and, even when it is not invited, they have poorly developed skills of self-protection. No doubt the primary way they learned to protect themselves was to give others whatever they wanted. They say to themselves, "Maybe if I give whatever is expected they won't hurt me any more."

This trait leads codependents to perceive and treat themselves as objects that are designed for the use of others. They don't feel right unless they are being used or exploited by somebody else. They live for the well-being of everyone else and tend to lose themselves in the process.

Nurturing. Codependents love to nurture, support, and take care of others. Joyce would often refer to herself jokingly as "the mother of the world." The problem was that it wasn't funny. It was true. Her powerful need to care for others became an obsession and a compulsion. She constantly focused on caring for others until she became so dysfunctional she could no longer care for herself.

How Counterdependents Lock into Other-centeredness. Counterdependents love codependents' other-centeredness. They are self-centered and need people who will make them the center of their lives. Codependents are good at this. Codependents need to act as mirrors in order to feel good about themselves. Counterdependents need someone to mirror back their strength and independence. As a result, the codependent and the counterdependent lock into each other in a very powerful way.

Intrusive and Receptive

Counterdependents are intrusive. They frequently invade the privacy of others without even thinking about it. They believe they are entitled to special or private access so they think they deserve to be close whenever they want to be.

Codependents are so receptive they lack boundaries. They don't know where they stop and other people begin. As a result they are willing to let other people invade their privacy. They don't get offended when others want to get too close. They are used to merging with others and getting abused in the process. They become uncomfortable and feel abandoned when forced to set limits and create reasonable boundaries.

To feel normal counterdependents need to invade someone's space while codependents need to have their space invaded. As a result there is another unhealthy match that locks the two players together in an addictive relationship.

This entanglement between intrusiveness and receptiveness forms the fourth lock that binds the counterdependent and the codependent. Study the following diagram for a moment.

Intrusive		*Receptive*

Rigid
  Boundaries
	. . .	*Lack of*
		  Boundaries

Well Defended	. . .	*Poorly Defended*
Aggressive	. . .	*Passive*

Let's take a look at each of these traits in more detail.

Intrusive.

Counterdependents invade the privacy and personal space of others without even thinking about it. Their grandiosity makes them feel they have the right to get as close as they want to other people. Their extreme independence allows them to move in and invade the privacy of others without asking permission. Their self-centeredness makes them oblivious to the reactions of others as they invade their space. This intrusiveness is characterized by three traits: rigid personal boundaries, strong personal defenses, and aggressiveness. Let's look at each more closely.

Rigid Personal Boundaries. Boundaries are what separate us from other people. Our physical boundary is our skin which separates us from other people and the world around us. We also have psychological boundaries that allow us to maintain our concept of ourselves as separate human beings.

Counterdependents have rigid psychological boundaries that keep people at a distance. They are experts at keeping people away. It's very difficult to even get close to a counterdependent unless he or she wants you to.

Well Defended: Counterdependents are experts at "psychological karate." They know how to insulate and protect themselves emotionally from other people. They do it by building walls and depersonalizing others. One counterdependent put it this way: "I learned a long time ago that it's no fun to get hurt. I also learned it's a hurtful world and no one is going to take care of me but me. I learned to survive by learning not to get hurt. I don't make anything or anyone too important to me. That way if I lose, it doesn't hurt too much."

Aggressive. Counterdependents tend to go after what they want aggressively. They view life as a battle or a contest, and they are more than willing to compete. They have learned to invade other people's space to get what they want. They often do this with little or no consideration as to whether the other person is interested in sharing or giving them what they want.

How Codependents Lock into Intrusiveness. Codependents expect their space to be violated. In many ways they appear to view themselves as doormats who need to be used by others. They are used to this and feel it is normal and natural. As a matter of fact, many codependents equate love with an invasion of privacy: "Of course he (or she) pushed their way into my life. That only proves that he (or she) loves me." This trait can cause codependents to set themselves up to be victimized by others.

Receptive

Codependents are receptive. They lack personal boundaries. They don't know where they stop and other people start. As a result they let people get too close too fast.

One codependent woman had a history of having sex with men on the first date. They would come to pick her up, flirt with her, and she felt obligated to respond sexually before she even got to know them. It proved to be a major task for her while undergoing counseling to not have sex before the third date.

Codependents also get scared and anxious whenever personal boundaries begin to change. They are willing to let people get close, just as long as they are willing to stay close. But if they are not close to someone, they feel uncomfortable, abandoned, and alone. They are uneasy operating in life without incorporating another person into their private space.

This receptiveness is characterized by three major traits: a lack of personal boundaries, poor personal defenses, and passivity.

Lack of Personal Boundaries. Codependents are not sure where their boundaries stop and other people's begin. They have learned from early childhood that they don't have a right to privacy. As a result, they tend to let people get real close real fast.

Poorly Defended. Codependents are not skilled at self-protection. When others act aggressively against them, their major defense is to comply, to do whatever is necessary to please the aggressor, and then rationalize the incidence of abuse.

Passive. Codependents tend to be passive when it comes to taking care of themselves. They can be active and aggressive in caring for others, but when it comes to self-care, they are stuck in neutral.

How Counterdependents Lock into a Lack of Personal Boundaries. Counterdependents love the codependent's receptiveness and lack of boundaries. They can be invasive and intrusive without hearing any complaints. They can feel free to operate in their partner's space without being criticized, rejected, or punished.

The only feelings that counterdependents are interested in are excitement, passion, and intensity. All other feelings are "no good" because they hurt. Counterdependents communicate that "It's your job to turn me on. It's your job to excite me so I don't have to pay attention to any other feelings."

The Mirror Effect

The relationship of these traits can be understood best by thinking about mirrors. Counterdependents need mirrors to look into in order to see a reflection of themselves. Because they are secretly so unsure of themselves, they believe they need a mirror to prove they exist. Codependents need to act as mirrors reflecting back someone else's image. Without having someone to reflect, they believe they have no reason to exist.

This is the lock that binds them together. Counterdependents believe, "If I don't have someone else to be my mirror, I will die." Codependents believe, "If I don't have someone who will let me act as a mirror, I will die."

Chapter

Interdependence—The Foundation of Healthy Intimacy

Recovery is possible. No matter how counterdependent or codependent we are we can get better. Recovery starts with knowledge about healthy behavior. What do healthy people look and act like? What do healthy relationships look like? The answers to these questions are vital.

Healthy people are **interdependent.** They combine the positive traits of both the counterdependent and codependent without taking on the negatives. Counterdependents overidentify with their strengths and deny their weaknesses. Codependents overidentify with their weaknesses and deny their strengths. Interdependents identify with *both* their strengths and their weaknesses. They are comfortable with the strong, powerful parts of themselves. They are capable of using that strength and power without feeling frightened or guilty.

Interdependents also identify with their weaknesses. They accept themselves as fallible human beings and believe they have a right to have faults and weaknesses. They have a right to be tired and to have bad days. After all, it is human to have weaknesses. Nobody can be perfect at everything. Interdependents accept this weak side of themselves as normal and don't feel a sense of shame or guilt when thinking about their limitations.

Interdependents are able to practice the serenity prayer. They can truly say and mean the words, "God grant me the serenity to accept the things I cannot change, the courage to change the things I can and the wisdom to know the difference." For counterdependents, the serenity prayer is a bit different. They say, "God grant me the courage to change everything because I am capable of all things." Codependents modify the serenity prayer this way: "God grant me the serenity to accept everything that happens because I am powerless to do anything in life."

Interdependent people express balance in their personalities and life-styles. They accept themselves in both their strengths and their weaknesses. As a result, they feel whole and together. Counterdependents and codependents are rigid, inflexible, and fixated on either their strengths or weaknesses. They deny a large part of who they really are.

Interdependents act out four primary traits: security, cooperation, social interest, and flexibility. The following diagram shows the general path of growth for both counterdependents and codependents as they mature into healthy, interdependent people.

Interdependents maintain a flexible balance between the traits of counterdependents and codependents. As a result, a pathway for growth can be established.

The Shadow Self

Within each counterdependent and codependent there is a shadow self that has repressed traits of their counterpart. This shadow self is frightening, and whenever these traits come to the surface, counterdependents and codependents experience fear, shame, and guilt.

> *Within each of us is a shadow self—a private urge to act out an opposite personality style.*
>
> *Within the counterdependent lurks a hidden and feared codependent.*
>
> *Within each codependent lurks a hidden and feared counterdependent.*

In order to recover, each partner must learn to embrace his or her shadow self and practice counterbalancing traits. The end result will be the development of the healthier traits of interdependency.

When grandiose counterdependents consciously recognize their insecurity, their grandiosity is integrated into a sense of security. The same is true for their other traits. Extreme independence becomes **cooperation** when they focus on their dependency needs. Self-centeredness becomes **social interest** as they learn to focus on and appreciate other people. Intrusiveness becomes **flexibility** when they learn to become receptive of others.

The codependent also has a shadow self that hides repressed counterdependent traits. Codependents are frightened by this strong, self-centered, and intrusive side of their personalities. They attempt to deny and hide these traits. Whenever they come to the surface the codependent experiences fear, shame, and guilt. "I have no right to be strong!" they say. "If I keep feeling and acting strong, something awful will happen!"

In order to recover, codependents must learn to embrace their shadow self by recognizing and practicing counterdependent traits that counterbalance their codependency. The end result is the development of the healthier traits of interdependence.

When insecure codependents consciously try to embrace and experience their self-worth and grandiosity their insecurity is integrated into a sense of **security**. When consciously balanced with independence, extreme dependence becomes **cooperation.** In the same way, other-centeredness can become transformed into

66

social interest as the traits of self-interest and self-awareness are practiced. Receptivity when counterbalanced with assertion becomes **flexibility** in responding to others.

To become interdependent we must develop the counterbalancing traits of the shadow self. It is only when we recognize and accept both our strengths and our weaknesses that we can get close to another person while still feeling safe.

Because the interdependent personality style is necessary for healthy intimacy, let's look at its characteristics in more depth.

The Interdependent Style

The interdependent style is a mix of four traits: security, cooperation, social interest, and flexibility.

Security: The counterdependent is grandiose; the codependent is insecure. In recovery we learn to develop a reality-based sense of security as we get to know who we really are in our strengths and in our weaknesses. We can acknowledge and enjoy our strengths. We can learn to recognize and accept our weaknesses, and, as a result, we can grow. We can work at improving in our weak areas and ask others to help us to compensate for things we cannot do or are not good at.

This sense of security is based on a strong sense of self-esteem. People with self-esteem are self-confident. They know they can meet the challenges of life with the help of others. They also have worth. They believe that they are worthy of enjoying the good things that life has to offer them.

Cooperation. Counterdependents are extremely independent and cannot tolerate asking others for help. Codependents are so extremely dependent they get frightened when they have to act independently. Interdependent people, however, are cooperative. They know their strengths and bring those strengths with them into relationships. When appropriate, they can act on those strengths without fear, shame, or guilt. Interdependent people also know their weaknesses. They know what they are *not* good at, and they have no problem acknowledging their weaknesses and limitations. They are capable of asking for the help of others in overcoming those weaknesses.

As a result, interdependent partners can be strong and independent when it is appropriate or they can be weak and dependent when that is appropriate. They can be genuine in both their strengths and their weaknesses. They don't need to pretend they are something they are not.

Once there was a boy who was trying to cut the lawn. The lawn mower kept hitting a big rock that was buried in the ground. The boy tried everything he could think of to move the rock. He pushed on it, pulled it, dug a hole around it, and tried to pry it out with a stick and shovel. Nothing worked. Finally, in desperation he went to his dad who had been sitting and watching him struggle.

"Dad," he said, "I give up. I've done everything I can do but I can't move the rock. I quit."

His dad looked at him and said, "Son, you haven't tried everything. There is one more thing you can try to get that rock moved."

"What's that?" the boy asked.

The father smiled and said, "You can ask me for help. That's the one thing you haven't tried."

Social Interest. Counterdependents are self-centered—they ignore others while imposing their needs and expectations on them. Codependents are other-centered—they ignore their own needs while attempting to impose the needs and preferences of others upon themselves. Interdependent people are socially interested. They know their own needs and are interested in fulfilling them. But they are also interested in the needs of others. They are concerned and helpful—but only up to a point. Interdependent people refuse to sacrifice themselves totally for others. They will help others when it is not destructive to themselves. When it becomes self-destructive they stop helping.

Flexible (Responsive). Both counterdependents and codependents are rigid and inflexible. While they react to deeply entrenched mistaken beliefs, they do not respond appropriately to what is happening here and now.

Both act out their inflexibility although in different ways. Counterdependents intrude on others. They don't know any other way to get what they want. Codependents invite others to intrude on them. They are receptive to the point of being exploited because they don't know any other way to relate.

Interdependent people are flexible. They have a variety of ways of dealing with others. They are capable of asking directly for what they need and want. If threatened they are capable of becoming aggressive, intrusive, and intimidating but only so far as needed to protect themselves. They are also able to follow the lead of others and can be receptive to the wants and needs of others. When it is appropriate to do so they are capable of surrendering within the context of a relationship.

This flexibility allows for maximum self-protection. The ability to self-protect allows interdependent people to feel safe *and* close at the same time. This allows them to respond spontaneously to the needs of other people. They can ask for what they need and want, then relax and allow others to give and to take care of them. They are able to receive. If others start to exploit them, they can become assertive or even aggressive in order to protect themselves. This flexibility allows interdependent people to relate to others safely and effectively.

Chapter 5

The Recovery Process

Recovery is possible. Even people with extreme counterdependent or codependent traits can change. And by changing themselves they can learn to develop healthy relationships. Recovery progresses through a series of five stages. It starts with **recognition** of the relationship problem. This generally happens when one partner creates a crisis by confronting the other. This crisis motivates the couple to **get some help** in figuring out what's wrong. They get a handle on their problems by doing a thorough **inventory** of themselves and their relationship. Once they can see the problems they both can work at **change.** Perfection does not necessarily result, but the **outcome** is a balanced partnership.

Many of these steps are not easy. It takes courage and perseverance to move through them. But you don't have to stay trapped in an addictive relationship. There is a way out. Let's look at each of these stages in more detail.

Recognition

We must recognize that a problem exists before we can solve it. The first step in fixing a troubled relationship is to recognize that we have one. It's hard to say, "I have a relationship problem!" It's much easier to blame our partner. "He (or she) has a problem. I have nothing to do with it. If my partner would change, everything would be wonderful."

Both partners in addictive relationships feel victimized by the other. They don't think about how their behavior has hurt their partner. They only think about how their partner has hurt them. The process of blaming is different for the counterdependent and the codependent, however.

Counterdependents blame their partners for being weak, helpless, insecure, and incompetent. Steve put it this way: "I have to take charge and get pushy or Joyce would never do anything right. Sometimes I get angry but it doesn't seem to bother her. She just takes it and smiles. It's hard for me to know that what I'm doing is hurting her because she never tells me. That's not my fault. Why doesn't she let me know what she's feeling?"

Counterdependents are often blamed for all of the relationships problems. They're the overt villain—the obvious "bad guy." Because they're the "top dog" and appear to be one up, it's easy to believe it's all their fault and to forget about the role the codependent is playing.

Codependents outwardly appear to accept the blame for what is wrong with the relationship, but they secretly blame their counterdependent partner. "If he (or she) were more sensitive and understanding and less self-centered and angry, the relationship would be OK. It's not my fault that he (or she) is like that. I'm just doing my best to put up with it and keep from getting hurt."

It's hard for codependents to recognize that they're part of the problem and are responsible for hurting their partners. "How could I possibly have hurt him (or her)? They're so strong and I'm so weak! I could never do the hurting. I'm the victim, and it's not my fault." This isn't true. Codependents have a personality style that invites their counterdependent partners to victimize them. Instead of setting limits and protecting themselves, they act weak and helpless. Instead of giving honest feedback, they tell their partners what they think they want to hear. They also secretly try to control and manipulate their partner. They turn their partners into a self-help project and try to fix them without ever telling their partner what they are trying to do. This codependent behavior hurts the counterdependent partner and the relationship. The codependent partner is responsible for changing it.

Steve and Joyce began to "bottom out" in their relationship. It happened when Joyce got involved in a recovery group for adult children of alcoholics (ACA). She realized that she wasn't being honest in her relationship. There were many things about Steve and their relationship that she didn't like, but she refused to think about them or discuss them with Steve.

She wrote a list of everything she was unhappy with in the relationship. Then she had a panic attack. "I can't think like this! There's no way I can tell Steve what I've just written! I feel like I'm going to die!"

Just the process of thinking about her unhappiness and writing down a problem list scared her to death. She kept her list a secret for months. She was even afraid to tell her ACA sponsor that she had written it.

Even though she didn't tell anyone about it, writing the list changed her. Joyce became more aware of the problems in the relationship. When things happened that hurt her or made her unhappy, she could no longer just block them out. Writing the list had given her the gift of awareness. She was now aware of the problems, and when they happened she knew it.

Joyce tried to lie to herself about the relationship problems. "It's not as bad as it could be," she told herself. "It could be worse. As far as men go, Steve is a pretty good catch." But a quiet voice within her had now been activated. She knew she was lying to herself and it bothered her.

Steve wasn't satisfied with the relationship either, but he didn't know why. Joyce was meeting all of his needs—sort of. Well, when he got honest about it, he wasn't completely happy. The high-powered sex had tapered off. Although Joyce was still available, he couldn't get the highs he used to. Part of him blamed Joyce, but deep inside he blamed himself: "If I were a good partner the sex would be as good as it used to be. There must be something wrong with me!"

He began to get to know Joyce better, and it seemed like she was on a different wave length. The things that really psyched him up seemed to mean little or nothing to her. She tried to go along with them, but Steve could tell her heart wasn't in it. Steve didn't enjoy the things that turned Joyce on. Joyce would get excited about decorating the house or going out with friends he really didn't enjoy. He couldn't understand what motivated her. Sometimes it annoyed him but he usually wrote it off to her "strange tastes."

This lack of common areas of interest and excitement had an impact. Steve felt that Joyce wasn't really being honest with him, that she was playing a game or just going along to please him. This bothered him because initially he believed Joyce was getting the same kind of mind-blowing experiences from their relationship that he was. As time passed, he wasn't so sure.

Steve denied and rationalized his problems by blaming them all on Joyce even though privately he felt responsible. When he was with Joyce he would start arguments and criticize her. He would feel badly about it afterward but couldn't stop himself. Joyce would accept the criticism and verbal abuse and then, within an hour, bounce back to her normal, smiling self.

Steve couldn't understand this. "How could she not be upset by what I did?" he'd think. "She's lying to me. And if she hides her anger from me what else is she hiding?" He began to feel like he didn't know her.

Then it happened. Joyce finally got up the courage to read her "problem list" to Steve. She was scared to death and had to rehearse it in her head a thousand times before she was able to do it. As a matter of fact she was so scared that she had to stir up a pile of anger to give her the courage to do it. This wasn't hard to do because she had been pushing her anger down for months.

One evening she read the list to Steve. She put on her best detached recovery self and told Steve there was something she had to tell him. She took a deep breath and read the list.

Joyce told him that she thought he was a workaholic and that his work was more important to him than she was. "I feel like a second fiddle," she said. "You're working all of the time. You never have time for me except when you want to have sex. Sometimes I wonder if you love me or just want to make love to me."

Joyce went on to tell him that she often didn't enjoy having sex with him. "I know you enjoy it," she said, "so I do the best I can to please you. But you're too rough, too controlling, and too intense. It seems as if all you want is your own pleasure and you really don't care about mine."

Joyce also told him she was tired of listening to him and building his ego all the time. "Sometimes I think you're self-centered," she said. "You brag about yourself all of the time. You make grandiose and unrealistic plans and often you make a fool out of yourself by bragging about your glorious plans to our friends."

"Sometimes I feel like you don't need me or even want me in your life," she continued. "You're so independent that there isn't room for me. I want to be part of your life to share it. I don't want to be an appendage to a self-contained, professional working machine."

She capped the whole thing off by telling him that she thought he was intrusive, insensitive, and didn't really care about her. "I sometimes feel used," she said. "It feels like you're only interested in me when I tell you what you want to hear and do what you want me to do. And I'm tired of it."

Notice Joyce's four major complaints. She found

Steve to be grandiose, overly independent, self-centered, and intrusive—the major traits of a counter-dependent.

Steve was devastated. He couldn't believe what he heard. He thought they had the perfect relationship, but for the first time Joyce told him otherwise.

Disoriented and immobilized, he couldn't think. He felt as if he was floating out of his body. "What's wrong with me?" he thought. "I feel crazy."

He didn't know what to say, yet Joyce wanted to talk. He couldn't pull his thoughts together. He sat in silence, unable to move because of a combination of anger, shame, and confusion.

It took him several weeks to get his response together. Part of him knew Joyce was right. "I do have problems," he told his sponsor. "But so does she. She's blaming it all on me, and it's not all my fault. I'm willing to change, but I'm not going to accept the total blame."

Now it was Steve's turn. He wrote out a "problem list" and presented it to Joyce.

"I was really upset with the list you read to me," he began. "It hurt. In fact, it devastated me. I couldn't believe what I was hearing."

Joyce sat rigidily in a chair, scared to death. She expected Steve to either hit her or leave her. She knew, in her own mind, that she had destroyed their relationship.

"You criticized me for being grandiose. Well, I have to be. You're so insecure you never plan anything. It seems like you're afraid to take a risk or do anything out of the ordinary."

Joyce winced because she felt it was true. She held back her tears as Steve continued.

"You say you want to be independent, but I don't believe it. You depend on me a lot. When I try to tell you to get more independent you get mad. I don't include you in things because it feels like you're trying to smother me. It seems you want to be involved in everything that I do because you don't have a life of your own. But when you do get involved, you criticize my way of doing things. My way is never good enough. You want me to do it differently. It seems like you've made it your job in life to do a make-over on me."

Joyce was ready to cry, but she held it back. She wanted to hear what Steve had to say. There was also something deep inside her coming back to life. "He's not hitting me," she realized. "He's not leaving me or going crazy. He's actually talking to me." This was the last thing in the world she expected Steve to do.

"I get confused," Steve said. "I love you and I want us to be happy. I want our relationship to work. But it seems when I'm being me, when I'm acting the way I really want to act, when I'm doing the things that really turn me on, it seems that you don't like me. I feel like I have to be something that I'm not in order to make you happy, and I'm not willing to do that."

"You give me mixed messages all of the time. When you look unhappy and I ask you about it, you say everything is fine. I'll say something and you'll lock yourself away on the phone with your sponsor for an hour. I know you're mad at me but I don't know why. When I ask you about it, you say nothing is wrong. I know you're lying but I don't know what to do about it."

Steve was saying things he had thought privately for months but never had the courage to say. Joyce was in shock. She felt dissociated and exposed. She couldn't believe he knew so much about her.

"You tell me I'm too aggressive sexually. You've never told me that before. I thought you enjoyed it. You told me I was a good lover, and now all of a sudden I'm an insensitive monster. If you didn't like what I was doing, why didn't you stop me. Why didn't you tell me? How can I be responsible for your reactions when you act like everything I do is fine."

He then told Joyce that he felt she got overly involved with people. "You sacrifice yourself to others, and your friends take advantage of you. They use you and you let them. Then you get angry with me when I tell you to stand up for yourself."

Steve felt like crying because he was hurting so badly. He felt alone. He wanted to get close to Joyce but didn't know how. "It really hurts to think that you just put up with me. It hurts me to see you let other people take advantage of you. I thought we had a good thing and now you tell me that you just tolerated me and the things I did."

Notice Steve's major complaints. He felt Joyce was insecure, overly dependent, other-centered to the extreme of being a martyr, and receptive to the point of pretending that she liked things that she really didn't like. These are the traits of a codependent.

Now they had it all out on the table. They both knew that something was wrong, but neither of them knew exactly what it was. Both were willing to try to fix it. But they each felt a growing sense of inertia, as if some powerful, irrational force was holding them back. This force is called resistance.

Why are we resistant to change? Why is it that one part of us can be tired of the pain and willing to do anything to get well while another part of us actively sabotages our recovery? The resistance comes from an irrational fear that we will die if we change.

We developed our codependent or counterdependent style as children. These roles were necessary for our survival. We needed to act in those ways to cope with the neglect or abuse we received as children. This became the only way we could cope with life. As a result, we kept acting out those traits as adults because we believed we would die if we stopped.

It wasn't a rational decision—it was an emotional one. But we don't even realize we've made it until we try to change our behavior. When we try to change, we become confused and panic. Something feels horribly wrong, so we run back into the coping behavior that has worked in the past. We reactivate our counterdependent or codependent styles.

Steve was counterdependent and knew it. He knew his self-centeredness was a problem, and he decided to change. But when he tried to stop being self-centered, he felt a sense of panic. His heart started pounding and he got scared. It was irrational, but he felt a sense of fear whenever he started to get interested in others.

Joyce had a similar problem. As a codependent Joyce always focused on others. She realized that she had lost herself in Steve and decided to change. She tried to focus on herself instead of Steve. But thinking about herself was scary. Fear built up inside her. To stop the fear she had to start taking care of someone else. She was amazed at how caretaking for Steve could make her fear go away.

Both counterdependents and codependents will feel fear or terror when they first experiment with behaviors related to their shadow self. This is why they need help to change. They need to talk with others who have been there and have recovered. They need to see that change *is possible* and be willing to get help.

Getting Help

Fixing a troubled relationship is a tough process. We can't always do it alone. Most couples need help in the form of new information, objective feedback, and a source of courage, strength, and hope to allow them to overcome their resistance to change.

Most people in troubled relationships don't know much about intimacy. Both Joyce and Steve knew something was wrong but they had no idea what it was. They knew they were hurting because of their relationship, and they both wanted the relationship to be better. They tried everything they knew, but nothing worked. They tried to talk it out and ended up arguing. Their relationship didn't get better. In fact, it got worse, and they began to feel hopeless. They didn't want the relationship to end but they didn't know what to do. They needed new information: their old ideas didn't work. Neither Steve nor Joyce knew exactly what was wrong or how to fix it.

To improve a troubled relationship we need new information. But where do we get it? Many of us start by going to family or friends. We talk with them about what is happening in the relationship. We see if they have experienced anything similar and have worked it out. But we're cautious. We realize that relationship problems often run in families and that we often choose close friends who are very much like we are. So we don't get surprised when our relatives and close friends have problems that are similar to our own.

Joyce talked with her mother who said, "I told you not to get involved with an alcoholic. I don't care if he's recovering or not. Once a drunk always a drunk. Of course he treats you badly. It's not your fault. Why don't you get out while the getting is good. Find a decent guy who doesn't drink and drug his life away. Don't make the same mistake I did with your father. I let him trap me. I should have gotten out when I was younger. Now I'm too old to change."

This advice didn't help. Joyce loved Steve and didn't want to leave. So Joyce called Gail, a friend of hers who belonged to Alanon, a support group for the spouses of alcoholics. Gail's husband was still drinking, but Gail seemed pretty happy.

Joyce described what was happening with Steve. Gail said, "Just 'turn it over' Joyce. Steve isn't such a bad guy. He's sober and in recovery. That's more than I can say about my husband. Be grateful. Lower your expectations and start to work on yourself. When you get your own life together, you'll learn not to expect too much from your relationship."

Joyce wasn't satisfied with this response either. "We've got a problem in our relationship. I know that, and I want to fix it. I don't want to leave and I don't want to settle for what I have. I want the relationship to get better."

We need accurate information if we want to fix a troubled relationship, and we generally won't get it from relatives and friends because they're not experts on relationships.

Once I had an electrical problem in my house. I called my brother-in-law, who makes his living as a bricklayer. He came over and worked on the electricity for six hours and then told me the problem was unfixable. He was very confident, saying he knew all about electricity and there was no way the problem could be fixed. I wasn't satisfied so I called an electrician. In thirty-five minutes he fixed the problem that my brother-in-law couldn't fix in six hours. Why? Because he was an expert electrician with accurate information and skills.

If you want to fix your relationship, get information from experts. Where do you get it? The first place is a bookstore. There are many good books on relationship problems and how to fix them. There are also audio and videotapes.

Joyce practically bought out the relationship section of the bookstore. She spent hours reading and finally thought she had figured out what was wrong. She told Steve about it, but he disagreed with her. They argued and Joyce felt like she was back at square one. What happened?

She had good information and tried to use it, but she got stuck. The problem was that Joyce was too close to her relationship to be objective. Trying to fix a relationship all by ourselves is much like trying to shave or put on makeup without a mirror. It can be done, but the outcome may not look very good.

What's the answer? We need someone who can give

us both accurate information *and* an objective, unbiased point of view.

One way to do this is to find other couples with healthy relationships and cultivate them as friends. Then we can find out how they handle their relationship problems. Remember, however, that friends and relatives are not trained counselors and may, with the best of intentions, give bad advice.

Where do you go to find couples who are healthy? Recovery support groups can be the answer. There are four Twelve Step Programs that focus on helping people understand and resolve their relationship problems. **Alanon** is helpful for people who are married to chemically dependent partners; **Adult Children of Alcoholics (ACA)** is designed for people who grew up in alcoholic or dysfunctional families and never learned how to have a healthy relationship; **Codependency Anonymous** and **Relationships Anonymous** are groups for people who have a tendency to get involved in dysfunctional relationships as adults. At these support groups you can find people who are well advanced in their personal recovery. Not only can they act as positive role models, but you can ask them to share their experience, strength, and hope with you as you recover. In this way unnecessary mistakes and setbacks can be avoided.

Be cautious as you get involved in support groups. After all, people go to support groups *because* they have problems. Some people recover faster than others. You'll find some excellent role models for recovery but you will also find some people with serious relationship problems. Just because someone has been around a support group for a long time doesn't necessarily mean that he or she has recovered.

There's an old AA slogan, "Stick with the winners." Be sure you get to know people in your group before blindly following what they tell you. Study the basic principles of the program. Learn all you can. Don't rely on any one person. Rely on the group conscience, the consensus of sincere group members working together for one another's recovery.

For many people, professional counseling can be a lifesaver. Marriage and family counselors are trained to help couples communicate more effectively and work together on changing. They have studied the common problems that couples have and they have learned effective problem-solving strategies to help resolve those problems. They know how to listen and give objective feedback. With professional counseling you can learn the fastest and easiest ways to resolve your relationship problems.

How do you know if you need a professional counselor? Sit down with your partner and try to work out your problems by yourselves. If you end up "running around in circles," then you probably need a referee. Most couples do. Relationship problems are caused by unconscious habits that are blindly repeated again and again. You may be so close to your problems that you can't see them, and even if you can see them you can't get out of them. The best referee you can get is a professional counselor.

Inventory

Once you know that you have problems, you need to

do a thorough inventory of yourself and your relationship to help clarify the problems.

Steve and Joyce worked together to inventory their problems. They used three categories: **my problems, your problems,** and **our problems.**

Steve identified two major problems caused by his counterdependence. He was **self-centered.** He didn't like it, but he knew it was true. He expected the relationship to center around his needs and wants. He would get annoyed or angry if Joyce ever wanted him to get involved in meeting her needs. He was also **extremely independent.** He wouldn't allow Joyce to help or support him. He would never share any feelings of weakness or vulnerability.

Joyce identified two major problems caused by her codependence. She could see her **insecurity** and what it was doing to the relationship. She realized that she rarely told Steve what her needs were. She just assumed that Steve wouldn't be interested. She recognized that she had no right to blame Steve for not giving her things that she never asked for. She was also aware of her **other-centeredness.** She was more than willing to lose herself in Steve. She enjoyed becoming obsessed with him. It was difficult for her to keep the focus on herself. This made it difficult for Steve to know who she really was. She was so busy being his mirror that she lost touch with herself.

Steve and Joyce agreed there were two major problems with the relationship. They both expected the relationship to provide **instant gratification.** Steve wanted instant excitement and intense sexuality and passion. Joyce wanted to feel affirmed, complete, and secure. They both had a tendency to lose their **boundaries** and get overly involved with each other to the exclusion of all other friends and activities.

They wrote down a problem list that looked like this:

Relationship Problems
1. *Instant gratification*
2. *Lack of boundaries*

Steve's Problems
1. *Self-centered*
2. *Extremely Independent*

Joyce's Problems
1. *Insecurity*
2. *Other Centeredness*

Once Joyce and Steve knew exactly what the problems were, they were ready to start solving them.

Change

The final step is to change—to start acting differently. It will be uncomfortable and scary at first, but with persistence it can be done.

The first change you have to make is to apologize to your partner for the hurts. That's called **making amends**.

Steve and Joyce sat down and started talking about their problems. Steve started the process. "Joyce," he said. "I love you. I really do! I know I've done things that hurt you. I know I've caused you pain and I'm sorry. I thought I was helping. Now I can see that I wasn't. The truth is I'm not always in control of what I do. When I get scared or feel weak and helpless I go on automatic pilot. My grandiosity and self-centeredness flair up. It seems like I have to invade your space and criticize you. I can see it's a problem. I know it hurts you. I'm sorry, and I want to work at changing it."

Joyce then said, "Steve, I'm part of the problem, too. I'm afraid to tell you how I feel because I'm intimidated by you. I always blamed my fear on you and used you as an excuse for not being honest and telling you things that I knew you needed to hear. My passivity has hurt you and it has hurt our relationship. I'm sorry and I'm willing to work with you to change it."

This amends process set the stage for change. It allowed both Steve and Joyce to put the past behind them, forgive, talk honestly, and resolve unfinished past experiences. The process gave them hope that their love was still alive. It helped them see that they both created the problem and that together they could resolve it. It affirmed to both of them that they were willing to work together.

The next step in changing is to **practice the traits of the personality style that is opposite to our own.** If we are counterdependent we must begin to consciously practice codependent behaviors. If we are codependent we must begin to practice counterdependent behaviors. Why? Because a codependent shadow self lives within all counterdependents and a counterdependent shadow self lives within all codependents.

In early recovery, we are terrified of that opposite shadow self. We believe that we will die if we acknowledge or act out the thoughts, feelings, and behaviors associated with the shadow self. It's not rational, but we still feel this way. When we consciously practice the traits associated with our shadow self we can learn to achieve balance. We can learn to interrupt the rigid all-or-nothing thinking that locks us into one style of thinking and behaving.

Counterdependent partners have to stop exaggerating their strengths and learn how to accept and communicate their weakness and insecurity. They must learn to recognize when they are being self-centered and consciously try to focus their attention on their partners. They also need to realize that their grandiosity is a cover-up for fear and security. They need to start telling their partners about their fears and feelings of weakness. They need to become aware of their extreme independence and learn how to depend on their partners and give their partners credit for helping them. Finally, counterdependent partners have to recognize their tendency to be intrusive. They have to back off and stop intimidating their partners by invading their privacy.

Codependents need to recognize they use their feelings of insecurity and weakness as an excuse to avoid recognizing and taking responsibility for their strengths and capabilities. They have to learn to recognize and act on their strengths. They need to recognize when they are insecure and learn how to challenge themselves: "Am I really unable to do this or am I just scaring myself out of trying?" They need to learn how to act in spite of the fear.

Codependents must recognize that their dependence

is simply a device to attribute their strengths to someone else. Once they are convinced that they need a powerful rescuer to function, codependents attribute all of their power to that person. They give away credit in spite of working hard and doing incredible things. Consequently, they have to learn to act independently and take credit for what they have done.

This requires codependents to stop being other-centered — making someone else the center of their universe — and learn how to focus on and care for themselves. They also need to learn how to set limits, to stop being receptive to all people at all times. They have to learn how to defend themselves against others when it's appropriate to do so.

The Outcome

Did it work? Were Steve and Joyce able to fix their relationship? The answer is yes and no. Yes, their relationship got better. No, it wasn't a perfect one.

Steve recognized and changed many of his counter-dependent traits. But during times of high stress he often relapsed back into grandiosity and self-centeredness. He still tends to be independent and has to work consciously at involving Joyce in his plans and projects. He learned how to share his feelings with Joyce. He learned how to get in touch with and communicate his fear and his pain while no longer hiding behind his strength and competence. He found he could rely on Joyce for love and care when he felt weak and helpless. And he discovered that he liked it. He learned he didn't have to feel ashamed or guilty for being a fallible human who got tired and needed the care of someone else.

Joyce became more tolerant of Steve's personality. She realized these tendencies were a part of him. He could soften them but probably would never change them completely. And so she stopped trying to change and control him. Instead, she realized she loved him in spite of—perhaps even *because* of—these traits. After all, she could never love a weak, compliant man. With Steve's new communication skills and his willingness to admit when he was wrong and apologize, Joyce was able to live comfortably with him.

She also changed many of her codependent traits. She recognized her anger and her core of power and strength. She learned to set limits and defend herself when others tried to invade her space or get her to do things that she didn't want to do. She learned how to love Steve without losing herself. She began to develop a life of her own with other interests. Although Steve was still important to her, she knew she could survive if he left her. She *wanted* to be with him; she no longer *needed* to be with him.

Joyce also had relapses. There were times when she felt frightened or insecure and she would turn to Steve although she really had the strength to deal with it herself. But she learned to be gentle with herself. She accepted these relapses into codependence as normal and learned to work her way out of them quickly.

Steve learned to be more tolerant of Joyce. With her newfound strengths he found it easier to respect and admire her. When she relapsed into being a victim and tried to manipulate and control him by acting weak and insecure, he no longer got angry. He accepted it as a normal, natural part of her personality and learned to gently confront and encourage her.

Steve and Joyce now had a partnership. They didn't have a perfect relationship because there is no such thing. They didn't merge and become one because that's impossible. But they did learn to share a life together. They learned that they were two fallible human beings moving along a strange, miraculous journey through life. They agreed to share that journey with each other.

They were willing to accept each other in their strengths *and* in their weaknesses. They were willing to love each other in spite of their faults and be tolerant and forgiving. They could give each other a loving "kick in the butt" when they needed it to grow and move ahead. They were able to support and love one another, surrendering the weakest and most vulnerable parts of themselves to each other.

Did they have intense, passionate, mind-blowing sex? Did Steve still "explode into a cloud of orgasmic dust"? Sometimes, but not always. However, their sexual experiences did develop a new gentleness and firmness. With a new found depth and joy, they became willing to surrender themselves physically to the ebb and flow of romantic love.

This led to a new sense of security for both of them. Steve and Joyce knew who they were and how to like themselves. As they learned to cooperate they knew what they were about as a couple. Their relationship was reciprocal—they both worked at it voluntarily. They honored their commitments and learned how to say "no" to each other and negotiate their differences. They found less and less need to be controlling as they learned to share power openly and honestly in an atmosphere of mutual respect.

A new level of social interest also developed. As they learned to "self-love," their love for each other grew. As they learned to trust their love for each other, they found a desire to share that love with others. They developed more friends who were closer and more enduring. They also learned the art of flexibility. Somehow, certain things weren't as important as they used to be. They learned to slow down and make time in life, to back off and see the other's point of view. They learned to experiment with new ways of doing things.

Steve and Joyce were able to do this because they found the core of strength and majesty that each of them possessed. And they knew that by sharing their strengths they could overcome their weaknesses. Together they could be more than they could ever be alone. They agreed to love each other forever—one day at a time.

A Final Word

Addictive relationships are real. They can happen any time two people experience intense passion and sexuality without sharing other values, experiences, and lifestyle preferences. The only thing an addictive relationship has to offer is that it makes us feel good *right now.* When it stops making us feel good there is a major crisis in the relationship because that was the only thing being shared.

My hope is that this book has helped you understand the players in the addictive relationship. Remember, it always takes two to play. The major players are the counterdependent and the codependent. Counterdependents are top dogs who exaggerate their strengths while denying their weaknesses. They generally need to be in a one-up position to feel comfortable. Codependents are underdogs who exaggerate their weaknesses while denying their strengths. They generally need to be in a one-down position.

As a result, there are powerful attractions between counterdependents and codependents. Counterdependents feel attracted to codependents because they are top dogs who need to surround themselves by underdogs who know their place. Top dogs spend a lot of time criticizing and victimizing others; they need victims who won't fight back.

Codependents feel attracted to counterdependents because they are underdogs who need an excuse for staying that way. They are willing to trade away their strengths and self-esteem if others will only care for them and make them feel good. The problem is that the only people who are usually willing to tolerate being in a relationship with someone who demands constant strength are counterdependents who need to persecute and exploit.

This can be seen clearly when we look at the primary traits of the counterdependent and the codependent. The counterdependent is grandiose and the codependent is insecure. The counterdependent is extremely independent and the codependent is extremely dependent. The counterdependent is self-centered and the codependent is other-centered. The counterdependent is intrusive and the codependent lacks personal boundaries.

These differences cause counterdependents and co-dependents to get trapped in problematic relationships. Even if they get out of a relationship with one destructive partner they invariably will select a different partner with similar if not identical traits.

Recovery is possible if we are willing to develop healthy interdependence. Interdependent people develop four primary traits: security, cooperation, social interest, and flexibility. Security results from an integration of grandiosity and insecurity. Cooperation results from an integration of independence and dependence. Social interest results from integration of self-centeredness and other-centeredness. Flexibility results from an integration of intrusiveness and receptiveness.

I hope this information has helped you understand these traits and how they lock together. With this knowledge you can begin to examine yourself and your current and prospective partners and ask an important question: "Am I getting ready to pick up another poisonous snake?"

Remember, there is hope. Change is possible. The first step is to recognize that you have counterdependent or codependent characteristics and to admit that these traits are causing relationship problems. The next step is to enter a recovery program and work at changing those characteristics.

Recovery is a process of change. It is possible to change, but it's not easy. It takes consistent work and effort. But if we ever want to find a meaningful, satisfying love relationship, we must change ourselves first. We can spend forever looking for someone to love. We generally don't find this person because our personalities make us inherently unlovable. We attract people who complement our self-defeating character-istics instead of loving us for who we really are.

Recovery begins when we stop spending all of our time looking for someone to love and start reinvesting our energies in becoming a person worthy of the love of other healthy human beings. First the self, then the pos-sibility of healthy love. First we must become people who are capable of loving ourselves. Then we can begin attracting other healthy people who have the capacity to love us for who we really are, instead of being at-tracted to our self-protective counterdependent and co-dependent roles. Self-examination, self-awareness, and change or repeating the cycle of destructive relationship addictions—the choice is yours.

Appendix 1

Addictive Relationship Trait Questionnaire
Part I: Self-Evaluation

Developed By
Terence T. Gorski
Copyright, T. Gorski, 1989

Instructions: The following questionnaire is designed to help you determine whether you tend to be counter-dependent or codependent in your relationship style. It is rare to find someone who is totally codependent or totally counterdependent. Most of us have a balance of both traits with a definite tendency to prefer one style more than the other.

Each question will force you to choose between two different answers. Select the answer that best fits you most of the time.

When in an intimate relationship I am most likely to feel...

1. a. powerful   b. ineffectual
2. a. self-confident   b. uncertain
3. a. self-important   b. insignificant
4. a. entitled to special   b. unable to get what
   treatment from my   I really need from
   partner   my partner
5. a. special   b. ordinary

When in an intimate relationship and a problem develops I tend to...

___B___ 6. a. trust my own ability to solve it   b. trust my partners ability to solve it

___B___ 7. a. distrust my partner's ability to solve it   b. distrust my own ability to solve it

___B___ 8. a. blame my partner for causing the problem   b. blame myself for causing the problem

When I think about myself I generally...

___B___ 9. a. overidentify with my strengths   b. overidentify with my weaknesses

___B___ 10. a. deny my weaknesses   b. deny my strengths

In a relationship I am more likely to...

___B___ 11. a. make demands on my partner   b. expect my partner to make demands on me

If my partner could give me only one of the following things I would like to get more...

___A___ 12. a. praise for what I have done   b. approval that tells me I am OK

I feel most fulfilled in a relationship when I can...

___B___ 13. a. relax and not have to pay attention to my partner's needs   b. intuitively sense what my partner needs and meet those needs without being asked

If both my partner and I had legitimate conflicting needs, I feel that the right thing to do would be to...

___14. a. take care of my needs first

b. take care of my partner's needs first

I feel better when my partner...

___15. a. takes care of me

b. allows me to take care of him or her

In relationships I tend to...

___16. a. get close to my partner while keeping myself safe

b. get close to my partner by making myself vulnerable

___17. a. not tell my partner things that could hurt me later

b. tell my partner everything even if he or she might hurt me because of it

___18. a. directly ask my partner for what I want

b. wait for my partner to give me what I want

Addictive Relationship Trait Questionnaire
Part II: Partner Evaluation

Instructions: The following questionnaire is designed to help you determine whether your partner tends to be counterdependent or codependent in his or her relationship style. Remember this is your impression of your partner. Ask your partner to complete a self-evaluation (Part 1 of this questionnaire) and then compare his or her answers with yours. Remember, it is rare to find someone who is totally codependent or totally counterdependent. Your partner probably has a balance of both traits with a definite tendency to prefer one style more than the other.

Each question will force you to choose between two different answers. Select the answer that best fits your partner most of the time.

When in an intimate relationship my partner is most likely to feel. . .

_____ 1. a. powerful   b. ineffectual
_____ 2. a. self-confident   b. uncertain
_____ 3. a. self-important   b. insignificant
_____ 4. a. entitled to special   b. unable to get what
          treatment from my   I really need from
          partner   my partner
_____ 5. a. special   b. ordinary

When in an intimate relationship and a problem develops my partner tends to...

_____ 6. a. trust his or her own   b. trust my ability
            ability to solve it   to solve it
_____ 7. a. distrust his or her   b. distrust my ability
            ability to solve it   to solve it
_____ 8. a. blame me for   b. blame self for
            causing the problem   causing the problem

When my partner talks about self he or she generally...

_____ 9. a. overidentifies with   b. overidentifies with
            strengths   weaknesses
_____10. a. denies weaknesses   b. denies strengths

In our relationship my partner is more likely to...

_____11. a. make demands on me   b. expect me to make
                                              demands on him or
                                              her

If I could give my partner one and only one of the following things, he or she would like me to give more...

_____12. a. praise for what they   b. approval that tells
            have done   them they are OK

My partner seems to feel most fulfilled in a relationship when he or she can...

_____13. a. relax and not have to   b. intuitively sense what
            pay attention to my   my needs are and
            needs   meet those needs
                                           without being asked

If both my partner and I had legitimate conflicting needs, my partner would probably feel that the right thing to do would be to...

____14. a. take care of his or   b. take care of my
         her own needs first   needs first

My partner seems to feel better when I...

____15. a. take care of him or   b. allow him or her to
         her   take care of me

In our relationship my partner tends to...

____16. a. get close to me while   b. get real close real
         keeping self safe   fast even if he or she
                                      gets hurt

____17. a. not tell me things   b. tell me everything
         that could hurt   even if could use it
         them later   later to hurt them

____18. a. directly ask for what   b. wait for me to give
         he or she wants   what he or she
                                      wants

Relationship Trait Questionnaire Scoring Sheet

Part I: Self Evaluation:

1. a = ✓   b = ___
2. a = ___   b = ✓
3. a = ✓   b = ___
4. a = ✓   b = ✓
5. a = ✓   b – ___

Subtotal 1:
a = 3   b = 2

6. a = ___   b = ✓
7. a = ___   b = ✓
8. a = ___   b = ✓
9. a = ___   b = ✓
10. a = ___   b = ✓
11. a = ✓   b = ✓
12. a = ✓   b = ___

Subtotal 2:
a = 1   b = 6

13. a = ___   b = ✓
14. a = ✓   b = ✓
15. a = ✓   b = ___

Subtotal 3:
a = 1   b = 2

16. a = ___   b = ✓
17. a = ___   b = ✓
18. a = ___   b = ✓

Subtotal 4:
a = 0   b = 3

Grand Total for Myself:
a = 5   b = 13

Relationship Trait Questionnaire Scoring Sheet

Part II: Partner Evaluation:

1. a = ___   b = ___
2. a = ___   b = ___
3. a = ___   b = ___
4. a = ___   b = ___
5. a =   b = ___

Subtotal 5:
a = ___   b = ___

6. a = ___   b – ___
7. a = ___   b = ___
8. a = ___   b = ___
9. a = ___   b = ___
10. a = ___   b = ___
11. a = ___   b = ___
12. a = ___   b – ___

Subtotal 6:
a = ___   b = ___

13. a = ___   b = ___
14. a = ___   b = ___
15. a = ___   b = ___

Subtotal 7:
a = ___   b = ___

16. a = ___   b = ___
17. a = ___   b = ___
18. a = ___   b = ___

Subtotal 8:
a = ___   b = ___

Grand Total for My Partner:
a = ___   b = ___

Interpretation: This questionnaire is designed to help you determine if you have a tendency to be counterdependent or codependent as well as your perception of your partner. It measures preference for either counterdependent or codependent behaviors in a relationship. It does not measure the degree to which those behaviors and preferences create dysfunction in your relationship.

PART I

1. **Grandiosity and Insecurity:**

   Subtotal 1 indicates your tendency toward either grandiosity or insecurity in a relationship. If you selected three or more answers of "a" you probably tend toward grandiosity. If you selected three or more answers of "b" you probably tend toward insecurity.

   A. According to this questionnaire I tend to be

   [✓] 1. grandiose.   [ ] 2. insecure.

   B. I ____ with what the questionnaire indicates.

   [ ] 1. strongly agree   [ ] 3. disagree
   [ ] 2. agree   [ ] 4. strongly disagree

2. **Independence and Dependence:**

   Subtotal 2 indicates your tendency toward either independence or dependence in a relationship. If you selected four or more answers of "a" you probably tend toward independence. If you selected two or more answers of "b" you probably tend toward dependence.

   A. According to this questionnaire I tend to be

   [ ] 1. independent.   [✓] 2. dependent.

B. I ____ with what the questionnaire indicates.

[ ] 1. strongly agree   [ ] 3. disagree
[ ] 2. agree   [ ] 4. strongly disagree

3. Self-centered and Other-centered:

Subtotal 3 indicates your tendency to be either self-centered or other-centered in a relationship. If you selected two or more answers of "a" you probably tend to be self-centered. If you selected two or more answers of "b" you probably tend to be other-centered.

A. According to this questionnaire I tend to be

[ ] 1. self-centered.   [✔] 2. other-centered.

B. I ____ with what the questionnaire indicates.

[ ] 1. strongly agree   [ ] 3. disagree
[ ] 2. agree   [ ] 4. strongly disagree

4. Intrusive and Receptive:

Subtotal 4 indicates your tendency to be either intrusive or receptive in a relationship. If you selected two or more answers of "a" you probably tend to be intrusive. If you selected two or more answers of "b" you probably tend to be receptive.

A. According to this questionnaire I tend to be

[ ] 1. intrusive.   [✔] 2. receptive.

B. I ____ with what the questionnaire indicates.

[ ] 1. strongly agree   [ ] 3. disagree
[ ] 2. agree   [ ] 4. strongly disagree

5. Counterdependent and Codependent:

Grand Total #1 indicates your tendency to either counter-dependent or codependent in your overall relationship style. If you selected nine or more answers of "a" your overall relationship style probably tends to be counter-dependent. If you selected nine or more answers of "b" your overall relationship style probably tends to be co-dependent.

A. According to this questionnaire I tend to be
   [   ] 1. counterdependent. [✓] 2. codependent.

B. I ____ with what the questionnaire indicates.
   [   ] 1. strongly agree   [   ] 3. disagree
   [   ] 2. agree   [   ] 4. strongly disagree

PART II

1. Grandiosity and Insecurity:

Subtotal 5 indicates your perception of your partner's tendency toward either grandiosity or insecurity in the relationship. If you selected three or more answers of "a" you probably tend to see your partner as being grandiose. If you selected three or more answers of "b" you probably tend to see your partner as being insecure.

A. According to this questionnaire I tend to see my partner as
   [   ] 1. grandiose.   [   ] 2. insecure.

B. I ____ with what the questionnaire indicates.
   [   ] 1. strongly agree   [   ] 3. disagree
   [   ] 2. agree   [   ] 4. strongly disagree

2. **Independence and Dependence:**

   Subtotal 6 indicates your perception of your partner's tendency toward either independence or dependence in a relationship. If you selected two or more answers of "a" you probably tend toward independence. If you selected two or more answers of "b" you probably tend toward dependence.

   A. According to this questionnaire you tend to see your partner as

   [ ] 1. independent.   [ ] 2. dependent.

   B. I ____ with what the questionnaire indicates.

   [ ] 1. strongly agree   [ ] 3. disagree
   [ ] 2. agree   [ ] 4. strongly disagree

3. **Self-centered and Other-centered:**

   Subtotal 7 indicates your perception of your partner's tendency to be either self-centered or other-centered in the relationship. If you selected two or more answers of "a" you probably see your partner as self-centered. If you selected two or more answers of "b" you probably see your partner as other-centered.

   A. According to this questionnaire my partner tends to be

   [ ] 1. self-centered.   [ ] 2. other-centered.

   B. I ____ with what the questionnaire indicates.

   [ ] 1. strongly agree   [ ] 3. disagree
   [ ] 2. agree   [ ] 4. strongly disagree

4. Intrusive and Receptive:

Subtotal 8 indicates your perception of your partner's tendency to be either intrusive or receptive in the relationship. If you selected two or more answers of "a" you probably see your partner as intrusive. If you selected two or more answers of "b" you probably see your partner as receptive.

A. According to this questionnaire I tend to see my partner as

[   ] 1. intrusive.   [   ] 2. receptive.

B. I ____ with what the questionnaire indicates.

[   ] 1. strongly agree   [   ] 3. disagree
[   ] 2. agree   [   ] 4. strongly disagree

5. Counterdependent and Codependent:

Grand Total #2 indicates your perception of your partner's tendency to be either counterdependent or codependent in overall relationship style. If you selected nine or more answers of "a" your partner's overall relationship style probably tends to be counterdependent. If you selected nine or more answers of "b" your partner's overall relationship style probably tends to be co-dependent.

A. According to this questionnaire my partner tends to be

[   ] 1. counterdependent. [   ] 2. codependent

B. I ____ with what the questionnaire indicates.

[   ] 1. strongly agree   [   ] 3. disagree
[   ] 2. agree   [   ] 4. strongly disagree

Appendix 2

Counterdependent	Codependent
Grandiosity	**Low Self-esteem**
• Powerful ⟵⟶	• Ineffectual
• Self-confident ⟵⟶	• Uncertain
• Self-important ⟵⟶	• Insignificant
• Entitled ⟵⟶	• Deprived
• One-of-a-kind ⟵⟶	• None-of-a-kind
Independence	**Dependence**
• Trust Self ⟵⟶	• Trust Others
• Distrust Others ⟵⟶	• Distrust Self
• Blame Others ⟵⟶	• Blame Self
• Overidentify with ⟵⟶ Strengths	• Overidentify with Weaknesses
• Deny Weaknesses ⟵⟶	• Deny Strengths
• Demanding ⟵⟶	• Complying
• Praise Seeking ⟵⟶	• Approval Seeking
Self-centered	**Other-centered**
• Insensitive ⟵⟶	• Oversensitive
• Selfish ⟵⟶	• Altruistic
• Exploitive ⟵⟶	• Nurturing
Intrusive	**Receptive**
• Rigid ⟵⟶ Boundaries	• Lack of Boundaries
• Well Defended ⟵⟶	• Poorly Defended
• Aggressive ⟵⟶	• Passive

SUGGESTED READING

The following books will help you explore further what it means to be an ACOA.

Ackerman, R. J. *Children of Alcoholics: Bibliography and Resource Guide,* 2nd ed. Indiana, Pa.: Addiction Research Publishing, 1985.

_____. *Same House Different Homes: Why Adult Children of Alcoholics Are Not All the Same.* Pompano Beach, Fl.: Health Communications, Inc., 1987.

Black, Claudia. *It Will Never Happen to Me.* Denver: Medical Administration Corp., 1982.

Brooks, Cathleen. *The Secret Everyone Knows.* San Diego: Kroc Foundation, 1981.

Cermak, Timmen. *A Primer for Adult Children of Alcoholics.* Pompano Beach, Fl.: Health Communications, Inc., 1985.

_____. *Diagnosing and Treating Co-Dependence: A Guide for Professionals.* Minneapolis: Johnson Institute Books, 1988.

_____. *Evaluating and Treating ACAs: A Guide for Professionals.* Minneapolis: Johnson Institute Books, 1988.

_____. *A Time to Heal: The Road to Recovery for Adult Children of Alcoholics.* Los Angeles: Jeremy P. Tarcher, Inc., 1988.

Cruse, Joseph R. *Painful Affairs: Looking for Love through Addiction and Co-dependency.* Pompano Beach, Fl. Health Communications, Inc., 1989.

Forward, Susan, and Joan Torres. *Men Who Hate Women & The Women Who Love Them.* New York: Bantum Books, 1986.

Glenn, Stephen H. with Jane Nelsen. *Raising Children for Success.* Fair Oaks, California: Sunrise Press, 1987.

Gravitz, Herbert L, and Julie D. Bowden. *Recovery: A Guide for Children of Alcoholics.* New York: Simon and Schuster, 1987.

Kritsberg, Wayne. *The Adult Children of Alcoholics Syndrome from Discovery to Recovery.* Pompano Beach, Fl.: Health Communications, Inc., 1985.

Larsen, Earnie. *Stage II Relationships: Love Beyond Addiction.* San Francisco: Harper & Row, 1987.

Lewis, David C. & Carol N. Williams. *Providing Care for Children of Alcoholics: Clinical & Research Perspectives.* Pompano Beach, Florida: Health Communications, Inc., 1986.

Norwood, Robin. *Women Who Love Too Much: When You Keep Wishing and Hoping He'll Change.* Los Angeles: Jeremy P. Tarcher, Inc., 1985.

Schaeffer, Brenda. *Is It Love or Is It Addiction?* Center City, Minn.: Hazelden, 1987.

Subby, Robert. *Lost in the Shuffle: The Co-Dependent Reality.* Pompano Beach, Fl.: Health Communications, Inc., 1987.

Whitfield, M.D., Charles L. *Healing the Child Within: Discovery and Recovery for Adult Children of Dysfunctional Families:* Pompano Beach, Fl.: Health Communications, Inc., 1987.

Wegscheider, S. *Another Chance: Hope and Health for the Alcoholic Family.* Palo Alto, Ca.: Science and Behavior Books, 1981.

Woititz, Janet Geringer. *Adult Children of Alcoholics.* Pompano Beach, Fl.: Health Communications, Inc., 1983.

_____. *Struggle for Intimacy.* Pompano Beach, Fl.: Health Communications, Inc., 1985.

Other recommended resources from Herald House/Independence Press

GETTING LOVE RIGHT
Learning the Choices of Healthy Intimacy
by Terence T. Gorski

Designed to effect change, this book offers more than theory—it provides the skills to develop healthy relationships. Terence Gorski's comprehensive course on intimacy features models and guidelines that have already helped thousands. Gorski addresses such important questions as:
. **Are my standards realistic?**
. **How do I know when to make a commitment?**
. **How do I choose a healthy partner?**
. **How do I go about meeting my sexual needs in a time when AIDS is a risk?**
Self-assessments and questionnaires at the end of each chapter help readers apply principles and practical skills to their own lives and, by renouncing old patterns, move toward true, healthy intimacy.
52-2901-4

GETTING LOVE RIGHT
Videotapes
Tape 1: *Personal Growth for Healthy Intimacy*
55-0948-3
Tape 2: *Partner Selection*
55-0949-1
Tape 3: *Relationship Building*
55-0950-5
Set of three videotapes:
55-0951-3
Audiotapes
Tape 1: *Personal Growth for Healthy Intimacy*
55-0952-1
Tape 2: *Partner Selection*
55-0954-8
Tape 3: *Relationship Building*
55-0955-6
Set of three audiotapes
55-0956-4

ADDICTIVE RELATIONSHIPS
Why Love Goes Wrong in Recovery
by Terence T. Gorski

Terry Gorski answers vital questions about intimacy and recovery. What is normal in a love relationship? How do we build healthy, intimate relationships into our recovery program? Using a generous mix of humor and self-disclosure, Terry describes the different levels at which relationships operate. He explains the seven characteristics of addictive intimacy and why they feel so good in the short run and hurt so badly in the long run. He gives hope by describing the characteristics of healthy intimacy and provides guidelines for relationship building and transforming in recovery.
17-0226-2 booklet
17-0156-8 audiotape

RELATIONSHIP BUILDING AND TRANSFORMING
The Levels of Platonic and Erotic Love
by Terence T. Gorski

This is an edited transcript of Terry Gorski's one-day workshop on Intimacy and Recovery conducted on August 3, 1991, at the Fashion Institute of Technology in New York City. In this series Gorski describes the crisis of intimacy and the reasons why millions of Americans are experiencing problems in their love relationships.

He describes compulsive, healthy, and apathetic relationship styles and the five levels of relationship building—acquaintanceship, companionship, friendship, romantic love, and committed love. He also describes the levels of erotic relationships, including attraction, flirtation, sensual involvement, and sexual involvement. The final section explains the basic principles of intimate communication which are necessary to make this information work in the real world of relationships.
17-0224-6 (book)
17-0225-4 (four audiotapes)